Forever Changed

One family's triumph over tragedy through prayer and trusting in God's Word

Ranae D. Krull

WESTBOW
PRESS

A DIVISION OF THOMAS NELSON

ISBN: 978-1-4497-7085-3 (sc)
ISBN: 978-1-4497-7086-0 (e)
ISBN: 978-1-4497-7087-7 (hc)

Library of Congress Control Number: 2012918846

WestBow Press books may be ordered through booksellers or by contacting:

WestBow Press
A Division of Thomas Nelson
1663 Liberty Drive
Bloomington, IN 47403
www.westbowpress.com
1-(866) 928-1240

Printed in the United States of America

WestBow Press rev. date: 10/12/2012

To my incredibly resilient family. My best friend and husband, Randy; my blessings: Tony, Kayla, Isaiah, and Stacey. Our blessed additions of Bailey and David. Grandchildren: Kinnick and now Tinley. LORD JESUS: You are the BEST!

Forward

When Ranae asked if I would write a Forward for *Isaiah's Story*, the English teacher in me reflected on the themes and motifs that stayed with me as I read through her manuscript. In many respects, hers is a story that is played out in various forms a thousand times a day in hospitals across our country. Indeed, much of it brought back memories of my own family's faith being tested as we earlier sat and slept in the waiting rooms of some of the same hospitals that she writes about. And during that time we met other families whose own stories could fill volumes with their experiences.

So besides the fact that my own life would eventually weave its way into this story, I asked myself what it was that made me find her story special. Why did I wish that it had been available to me and my family when we found ourselves camped out in intensive care units with a fearful future ahead of us?

Ranae and her family put their whole trust in God and in their Lord, Jesus Christ. They prayed that His will would be done and were willing to accept whatever that meant for their son. As they prayed, thousands joined them in prayer over the weeks and months to follow. And what becomes so evident in the book is that God "spoke" to Ranae and her family, answering those prayers in so many different ways.

Sometimes He spoke to them as a calming presence, giving them the strength to emotionally deal with the critical days and occasional setbacks. Sometimes He spoke to them in the form of sending just the right person their way when they needed support or didn't know where to turn. Sometimes He spoke to them through the miracle of healing as Isaiah's condition improved beyond what many had predicted. Sometimes He spoke to them through the lyrics of a song.

But always He spoke to them through His Word, and not only did the many scripture passages bring them peace and hope, but they shared them with others whom they met in the hospitals or who followed their care pages. And what a glorious day it was when Isaiah was able to add his own testimony to the care pages along with the scriptures that inspired him.

Then I realized that the book's message of hope and comfort through prayer and God's Word was a message that transcended hospital walls. It could serve as a revelation and inspiration for people who knew that they needed more to rely on than the support of professionals, friends, or family to get through any of their tough times.

Now Ranae shares those Bible verses with others as they read about her son's tragedy and triumphs in *Isaiah's Story*. For people facing trials in their own lives, the verses can remind them of God's promise to be with us and care for us always until one day we will live with Him forever in new bodies absent of pain or imperfections. And for people who have never known that kind of assurance, a number of the scriptures mentioned in the book can show them the way of salvation and help them begin a personal relationship with a Savior who died so that they might live.

I never knew Isaiah or his family before his accident, but I feel so privileged to have played a part in his recovery. I frequently prayed that God would grant me the wisdom to know how to help him, and I felt that God spoke to me too and inspired my efforts. I also found myself opening my Bible more often and saying simply, "Word of God Speak."

I have never doubted that God has a plan for Isaiah. God gave him back his voice, and Isaiah continues to share his story and his faith with others. May Isaiah's story either help to start you on your faith journey or inspire your existing faith as much as it has my own.

Kathy Whitney
Isaiah's teacher, tutor, and friend

Acknowledgements

I'm sure there are many who could write a similar story about a trial you or a family member has faced. I felt God leading me to write our story, not only for the purpose of getting it all written down to share with our own family but to inspire and encourage all who are faced with trials.

Isaiah's life has changed so much and his desire is to share what has happened to him and how his God is more than able to sustain our faith during trying times. We can be sure of one thing, in this life we will have tribulation but we are to be of good cheer because Jesus has overcome. He is the One who has overcome and is able to hold us up under our trials.

I want to thank my husband and children for encouraging me to write this book. It has helped me get all my feelings down on paper and realize just how blessed we have been to have so many wonderful people holding our family up in prayer.

The doctors and nurses who cared for Isaiah while he was in Iowa City were beyond exemplary, they cared. I can't thank them enough for all they did not only for Isaiah but for our entire family. They provided us with valuable resources to help us understand what we were facing. One such tool was the <u>Acute Brain Injury</u> booklet printed by the University of Iowa Children's Hospital Center for Disabilities and Development. This booklet explains the Glascow Coma Scale and the Rancho levels of Cognitive Functioning. It helped us learn what to expect and understand more about severe brain injury.

You can read all the blogs and comments on Isaiah's carepages by going to <u>www.carepages.com</u> and registering as a member. Then you can type in isaiahkrull and view his page and photos we posted. I have only written a few of the blogs in this writing but you can review it in it's entirety online.

My prayer is that no one will walk away from reading this book and not be encouraged. We have tasted and found the LORD to be more than we could've imagined. He has and will continue to sustain us in our daily lives until the Day He returns to take us to our eternal home. Don't let this opportunity to accept what He has done for you pass you by. Trust in the work He did on the cross for you. He wants to have a relationship with you, it's up to you to choose Him. Isaiah was only sixteen years old and that day could've been his last on this earth. He already had a relationship with Christ and would've gone to be with Him that day. Don't let this opportunity today pass you by for you do not know what the day holds for you. *For* no *eye has seen, no ear has heard, no mind has conceived what God has prepared for those who love Him (1 Corinthians 2:9).*

I thank the LORD for each of you and what He will do. All for His glory.

Chapter One
The Call

I'm looking across the room, watching my 20-year-old son change his 19-month-old nephew's diaper. I smile as Isaiah tries to hold the baby's legs, wipe and get the new diaper on before any more accidents happen. Any mother might find this a fun scene, but it is especially enjoyable for me since Isaiah should not even be alive to do things like this. I feel incredibly blessed because not only do I get to enjoy being a new grandmother, but I still have the privilege to savor moments like this with Isaiah.

To play "peek-a-boo" with his nephew and to sing along as a favorite song comes on the radio may seem like such simple things, but not to Isaiah. Only three-and-a-half years ago he was not able to talk or walk or even eat on his own let alone play or sing.

That was the summer that would change our lives forever and also teach us what it really means to trust in Jesus Christ completely. Verses from Isaiah 43:1-3 would hit the mark and comfort us as we watched our son, Isaiah, struggle for life: *"But now, this is what the LORD says–he who created you, O Jacob, he who formed you, O Israel: Fear not, for I have redeemed you; I have summoned you by name, you are mine. When you pass through the waters, I will be with you, and when you pass through the rivers, they will not sweep over you. When you walk through the fire, you will not be burned; the flames will not set you ablaze. For I am the LORD, your God, the Holy One of Israel, your Savior."* We would learn what it means to pass through the "fire of trials" and not have it completely consume us. This season in our lives would only prove to strengthen our faith in our God who carries His hurting ones in His arms when all around is a raging river, waiting to sweep us away.

The hot, muggy month of July, 2008 was a summer of changes in the Krull household. Our oldest son Tony had moved back to our rural home south of Shell Rock while he finished working as a county deputy. He was soon to begin work as a police officer in nearby Waverly after he finished his police academy training and living at home would help him save some money for a down payment on a place of his own. Plus, initially it would be closer to his work.

Our second child, Kayla, was transitioning from community college to the University of Northern Iowa in Cedar Falls. Although we don't live far from the campus, she had chosen to get an apartment to completely experience college life. Yet she was still close enough to pop over when she wanted to catch up with the family.

Then there was Isaiah, who was preparing for his rapidly approaching junior year of high school. He had been lifting all summer with his football team, and football camp was only weeks away. He was sixteen and working several jobs that summer to earn some spending cash. He had been getting plenty of ribbing from his older siblings, who reminded us that they had worked when they were his age. I guess Isaiah had decided to play catch up by taking on several jobs.

Stacey, our youngest, faced the exciting new world of high school with some apprehension, but she was counting on her older brother looking out for her. She had already enjoyed a few weekend basketball tournaments with some of the high school girls and was getting to feel a little more comfortable with them.

Several years have passed since that summer and yet, as I reflect back, it seems it was just a few weeks ago. Life had been flowing by quickly that summer, and yet I had been savoring all the little things, like spending time camping with dear friends; boating at Uncle Monte and Aunt Kelly's cabin and being excited for Tony's first "real" job.

Then came the last weekend in July—it had started with Isaiah coming home from directing videographers at our church. His job was to sit in the back room, with head phones on and direct the camera operators out front as to when to zoom in on the pastor or which camera was live next. My quiet son enjoyed this volunteer position as it put him in the back and away from having to talk to many people.

On that Saturday night Isaiah was catching us up on everything he had been doing, including being promoted to clean-up crew on his detasseling job. He explained that this meant that after the rest of the crew had gone through a field and pulled the tassels off the tops of the corn stalks, he and a few of his friends would come through and catch any stragglers that had been missed. He was excited about this because it meant he would get paid more per hour.

Isaiah had always been a goal setter and would work extremely hard to make these goals come to fruition. He was the strong, silent type. One might call him a strong type-A personality. Not a person of many words, but he always stood strong for what he believed in even if it didn't line-up with the so-called majority. This was also true of his faith. He was not afraid to speak up when faith issues were addressed whether at biology class or in government class.

I have noticed that daughters are much better at coming home and giving all the details of the events that have gone on during their day. When Stacey walked in the door that Saturday evening, I knew we would get a moment-by-moment summary of her weekend at a basketball tournament she had participated in at Creighton.

Stacey, all smiles, proceeded to tell us how well their team had done in their games. She was able to start as the point guard and enjoyed the competition at this tournament. Isaiah and I, along with Randy, my husband, were enjoying a snack as we listened. Randy and I laughed at the boating stories with the basketball girls that Stacey was sharing, and we praised the hard work Isaiah was doing out in the fields.

It was getting late, and we decided we all needed to get some rest. The next morning was Sunday, and we would attend the 9:00 a.m. worship service. Isaiah had already gone to the Saturday night service, so he would not be going with us. He informed us he had his lunch packed already for his 4:00 a.m. take-off to go detasseling. He told me I would not have to get up with him, but I planned on getting up anyway to get my usual hug before he left.

The alarm buzzed at 7:00 a.m. Randy rolled over to make sure I was awake before he went down to shower. I shot up and realized I hadn't heard Isaiah leave that morning, so I went to his room only to find it empty. He had gotten himself up and off to work already. Good boy! But I hadn't gotten a hug!

It was one of those perfect summer mornings in Iowa. The sun was shining brightly through the upstairs windows, and the sky was a bright blue. I love mornings like this, when I wake up to the birds singing in the grove nearby, and a fresh breeze flows through the windows. Summers in Iowa are also humid, and this day was no different.

When we arrived at church, our daughter, Kayla, and her boyfriend, David, were already there, saving us a seat. She was a server at Famous Dave's restaurant and had to work at 11:30 that morning, so it worked out for them to go to the first service with us. They would just need to leave as soon as the service was done.

As we walked out of the service, a dear friend, Dave, came up to us, his cell phone up to his ear. He said he needed to talk with us at once. He seemed shaken up a bit, and we wondered what was wrong. His son was on the same detasseling crew as Isaiah, and it was his son he was talking to on the phone.

He told us the boys had been in an accident. My first thought was *How bad can it be? Maybe someone got cut by the corn knives.* His son was explaining everything as it happened, but he was giving mixed reports. He told his dad that Isaiah and two other boys were in a car following the detasseling bus, and had been badly hurt. Then he said, "No, I think they are all out of the car and walking around."

About this time Randy's phone was vibrating, and he took the call. It was the detasseling crew leader, who also happened to be Isaiah's football coach. In a calm voice, he told Randy there had been an accident, that it was bad, and we needed to get to the local hospital as quickly as possible. He said EMTs had been working on Isaiah and a helicopter had just left, transporting him to the hospital.

Tony, had just arrived and stopped to see us before he attended the second service. He heard the news that Isaiah had been injured and wanted to go with us. The administrative pastor took notice of the group now forming around us and came over to see what was going on. We told him three young men had been injured, and we were not sure how serious all the injuries were, but that we knew that Isaiah was injured bad enough to be air lifted to Covenant Hospital. He assured us he would immediately inform the congregation to lift up these boys in prayer.

At the time, all I could think of was that the more people that could pray for these boys the better. I grabbed my cell phone and began sending out a massive text to everyone on my contact list, thankful that Kayla had taught me how to text! I was having a hard time concentrating because I was shaking so badly, but I knew I had to get this text sent off.

This had been one of those calls you never hope to get as a parent. I had often tried to imagine how I would react if that call ever came for us, but I don't think any of us really knows until it happens. I remember feeling numb at first and then trying to compose myself for Stacey and Tony. I took deep breaths and tried to calm myself. Still, I had all I could do to keep myself from shaking.

Randy, Tony, Stacey, and I took off in our car to head directly to the hospital which was approximately ten miles away. This is when I started to cry. Somehow I sensed we would not receive good news when we reached the hospital. I really didn't know what to expect except that it was going to be bad, or worse—he would be gone. Was I going to lose one of my children? What were Isaiah's last moments? Was he in pain? These were the questions that were flying through my head as Randy drove. All I could do was pray, and even that was difficult as I did not know what to pray for.

I would later find out that the timing of the text messages I had sent out had found their way to several of our friends before they left their own churches morning worship. Once they received the text, they gathered to pray for us and for the boys. I knew there were many praying for us because before we even reached the hospital, I was sensing a calm come over me. I trusted my heavenly Father to give me the strength and courage I knew I was going to need.

We were within view of the hospital when we saw a helicopter fly over the highway. Randy commented, "That is probably Isaiah in there." I strained my neck to watch it for as long as I could, all the while wondering what was happening with Isaiah. We could not get there fast enough. Although I knew there was nothing I could do at this point for my son, I just wanted to be there and let him know we were there with him.

By the time we parked, Stacey had gotten hold of Kayla and David who were pulling in at the same time. We reported to the nurses' desk that we were the parents of the young man just flown in. Then came the frustrating part—we had to supply her with our insurance card and fill out some papers. I was screaming on the inside, *"Are you kidding me?!"*

We were told to step into a side room until the doctor was able to speak with us. He came in, sat down, and looked us in the eyes. The doctor informed us that Isaiah had been given a paralytic drug to keep him from moving, that he had a severe head injury, a possible ruptured right eye, and a possible broken neck. Shock waves shot through my body. Was I hearing him right? Was Isaiah going to live? Was this truly happening to our family? I wanted to see Isaiah and tell him we were there. The doctor informed us his injuries were more serious than what they could handle at their facility, so they were preparing to air lift him to a larger hospital in Iowa City. He said we could see him briefly before they took him.

As we all entered the emergency room, I could sense both a feeling of calm and of strength fill me. I knew I had to be brave and strong, not only for Isaiah, but also for Randy, Tony, Kayla, and Stacey, who were all dealing with their own emotions. I just kept asking God for strength to help me deal with whatever was coming ahead.

There were so many people in the room working on Isaiah, but they stepped aside long enough for us to kiss him and tell him we were praying and that Jesus was with him; he would not be alone. From the outside his injuries did not look too severe. There was a two to three-inch cut above his right eye and he had a breathing tube down his throat. His eyes were shut and he was not moving. They had a neck collar on him; he was lying on a straight board, and I noticed some dried blood by his right ear. We thanked the hospital staff for all they were doing to help him and left the room.

While we were with Isaiah, the other two boys involved in the accident had arrived by ambulance. We walked into the next two rooms to see how they were doing. I really felt I needed to tell Isaiah's friend, Jordan, who was the driver of the car, not to feel guilty that it was an accident. When we entered the room Jordan was crying and kept saying he was sorry. We hugged him and went to see Isaiah's best friend, Cody, who was a passenger in the front seat of the car. He was conscious and also told us how sorry he was. The doctors were unsure about the extent of Cody's injuries, so we were not allowed to stay too long.

When we walked out of the emergency room, the waiting room was filled with our friends and family who were there to support us in whatever way we needed. I was overwhelmed! They not only offered to drive us to the hospital in Iowa City but gave us money since we didn't know how long we would be there or what our needs would be once we got there.

Greg drove Kayla's car with her, David, Tony, and Stacey as passengers, while Kent drove Randy and me in our car. Our objection that we could drive ourselves had been overruled, and once we were in the car, I was glad to be able to hold onto Randy and not have to worry about him driving. Of course, neither vehicle had enough gas, so we had to take the extra time to stop and fill them.

Kayla came over and asked if I would talk to Stacey because she wasn't acting like herself. When I walked up to the car, she was shaking and said she couldn't move her legs or fingers. I thought she was going into shock, so Randy told her to get in with us. I kept rubbing her fingers as Randy rubbed her back, trying to relax her and steady her breathing.

Stacey had become close with Isaiah since her two older siblings had moved on to college and work. She was really looking forward to having him there in high school to help her learn how everything worked, to protect her from the wrong kinds of guys, and just to have her big brother looking out for her. I knew she was afraid she was going to lose him.

My own thoughts were stirring as I asked God, "Why Isaiah?" He had always been a strong, Christian young man. He wasn't in the drinking crowd, didn't do drugs, and was bringing his friends to youth group with him. Why would a good God allow such a faithful young man to suffer like this? I was questioning God's goodness at this moment.

I had a misconception of what God's sovereignty and goodness was. Isaiah 14: 24 and 27 state: *"The LORD Almighty has sworn, 'Surely, as I have planned, so it will be, and as I have purposed, so it will stand'...For the LORD Almighty has purposed, and who can thwart Him? His hand is stretched out, and who can turn it back?"*

These are difficult verses to grasp, yet God wants us to know He sees the whole picture. Standing atop the Sears Tower in Chicago, you can see for miles around. You can stand on the east side and watch the ships and speed boats out on Lake Michigan. Then as you walk around to the north side, you can see Wrigley Field. The people look like ants and the cars like mere toys. From this bird's eye view you can see an accident several blocks away and understand that no traffic will be flowing through there anytime soon. You can also see the poor souls heading in that direction who don't realize they will have to be rerouted.

But God sees it all, from beginning to end. He knew exactly what was going to happen in the coming weeks and months. I did not. Although we might think it would be a wonderful concept to be able to see what lies ahead in our futures, I don't believe we could always handle the reality of what we'd see. I decided to trust that God knew what was best, and trusting in Him brought me added peace.

I was so grateful Kent didn't offer any words of advice or sympathy. He just drove and allowed us to think and feel whatever we were feeling at the time. All that kept popping into my head were the words to a song we had sung a few weeks earlier in church, *"He can move a mountain. My God is MIGHTY to SAVE. He is MIGHTY to SAVE..."* What was He saying to me? That Isaiah would be saved physically? Or, was it that my comfort was in knowing that as a little boy, he had prayed and accepted Jesus as his Savior and was going to be with Him now? Either way, Jesus was now comforting me in such a real and powerful way that there was no doubt in my mind He was there and would carry us through, no matter what the news would be when we reached Iowa City.

Behind us was a caravan of cars and vans of friends and family. They wanted to be there for us, and I was so grateful.. My dear friend Michelle, and her husband Todd, were right behind us, and I called her and told her of the song. She began to sing it to me, and I was overcome, knowing that Jesus would care so much to give me what I needed. He was so real to me at that moment. I glanced at the cars following us and thanked Him for such dear, close friends.

It was over an hour's drive to Iowa City, so we had a lot of time to think and talk. Stacey was calming down and breathing normally, and we started talking about the night before. Stacey wondered if she had hugged Isaiah before they headed off to bed, and I wondered the same thing. What were our last words to him? Would they be our last words ever? So many thoughts and fears, and yet why was I feeling so calm? It could only be the comfort of Jesus.

After we arrived in Iowa City, we were told to go to the emergency entrance because the doctor wanted to speak with us. Dr. Adam Jackson, the neurologist who had been assigned to Isaiah, came in and informed Randy and me that Isaiah did, in fact, have a severe, traumatic brain injury. He also had lacerations around his right eye, a crushed right cheek, and possible C1 and C2 fractures. He asked us to sign a form that would allow them to place a "bolt" into Isaiah's skull so they could measure the swelling that was taking place inside his head. If we didn't sign it, he would die.

We just looked at each other and said we would sign. What other choice did we have? After we signed the form, we came out to let everyone know what was going on. There were so many who had followed us there, and we were so thankful for the support. One of the friends offered to pray for Isaiah and us, and we gathered right in the middle of the emergency waiting room and prayed. I felt a bit numb and had this sense of being in a bubble where things were revolving around us, and yet we were standing still and sounds were muffled. I can still remember that feeling and that emergency room scene as if it happened yesterday.

We had only been there a half hour when we received news that Isaiah's best friend, Cody, had been transported to Iowa City after they discovered he had suffered a broken neck. He would need surgery and stay in Iowa City as well. Although I didn't want Cody to be hurt, it was a comfort knowing his family was there, and we could lean on each other as we walked the road ahead.

So now our journey into the unknown began. I had never known anyone with a brain injury, so I really didn't know what to expect. All I knew was that a "survival mode" had settled in on me, and my emotions were pushed farther back. I was now on a mission. Whatever it took to help my hurting son get back to normal was what I was going to do.

Chapter Two
Severe Traumatic Brain Injury

We had been told to go up to the Pediatric Intensive Care Unit because that was where they would send Isaiah as soon as they finished taking a CT scan of his head and had placed the "bolt" in his skull. This CT scan would be one of many over the next few days.

Our family, my parents, sister, niece, and several church members were standing in the hallway that led to the PICU (Pediatric Intensive Care Unit) when a group from a local church came walking towards us. They asked why we were there, and we told them about Isaiah. The leader of the church group asked if they could pray with us, to which we replied, "We will take all the prayers we can!"

They intermingled with our group and started praying a powerful prayer of deliverance for Isaiah, a young man they had never even met. The tears started flowing as I realized these were dear brothers and sisters in Christ, lifting up our son. I was moved to such a place that I began to get a glimmer of something powerful that God wanted to do, not only in me, but in the lives of others.

After they left, the doctor said we could go in a few at a time to see Isaiah. Our immediate family quietly entered the room. What a shock to my system to see him attached to so many machines. The room was kept cool and a cooling blanket lay under Isaiah to keep his body temperature down in order to slow his body functions. The slower everything worked, the less stress there would be on his brain, decreasing its swelling.

Our family embraced each other. We barely said a word, only held onto each other as we tried to take in the magnitude of the situation. Here in this hospital bed laid a 16-year-old, 215-pound football player, helpless, not even able to breathe for himself. Dried blood stained his right ear, his right cheek bone was crushed, and a laceration creased the area above his right eye. Encircling his neck was a neck collar, and a tube extended from the top of his head where they had shaved his hair in order to place the "bolt."

It is the most helpless feeling in the world for a mother when she is not able to kiss away the hurt and make it all better. I realized I had always felt like I needed to be in control, to be able to protect my kids. At this moment, modern medicine was doing what it could to save my son's life and there was absolutely nothing I could do--except pray. This would be the greatest thing I would learn: when people are at the very bottom, with no one or nothing else to turn to, they can lean heavily on Jesus. *Psalms 68:19-20: "Praise be to the Lord, to God our Savior, who daily bears our burdens. Our God is a God who saves; from the Sovereign LORD comes escape from death."*

Dr. Jackson had told us that the first 72 hours were the most critical and that the swelling in the brain was the highest priority. They would deal with his eye and cheek injuries after the swelling was under control and had placed him in a medical coma to keep him from moving around and further injuring himself. My brain whirled with unasked questions. What was Isaiah thinking about inside that injured head? Was he in pain? Did he know what had happened? Would he ever come out of this? Would I ever get to hear his voice again?

It was closing on midnight, and everyone else except our kids and Jordan, the driver of the car, had left the hospital. Randy and I walked out of Isaiah's room with excruciating headaches. As we were coming around the corner of the door leading out of the PICU, Randy asked the nurse sitting there if they had any drugs for us. It probably came out a little wrong, but we were looking for something to help with the headaches. The nurse was quick to dig into her purse and offered us some Tylenol. We were so grateful for the kindness of this nurse and the kindness of the nurse caring for Isaiah.

That night Tony, Kayla, Stacey, and Jordan slept on the chairs and couches in the family lounge. Randy and I refused to leave Isaiah alone, so we slept on the chair and couch in his room. We wanted to be there if anything happened. It was a restless night, drifting in and out of sleep. The sounds of the machines beeping and doing the breathing for Isaiah were hard to push out of my ears.

I'm not sure what time it was all I know is that I suddenly awoke to find several nurses and doctors scrambling about the room. Isaiah's intracranial pressure number had spiked to 38. It was supposed to remain under 20. They were working on him for several minutes and then as the number came back down, they one by one left the room.

First thing the next morning, Dr. Jackson informed us that they would need to perform a procedure to relieve the pressure inside Isaiah's head. This meant they would drill a hole in his skull and put in place a catheter to drain the spinal fluid to make room for the swelling brain. Without this procedure there was no place for the brain to go with the hard skull around it. The only place for it to go was down his spine which would mean death. If we didn't sign, Isaiah would most likely die. On the other hand, if we did sign, there was no guarantee he would live. The doctor assured us they would care for him as if he were their son or brother which was of great comfort to us. We signed.

It had been a long night. We were still in our church clothes from the day before, hadn't brushed our teeth, and needed to figure out how we were going to organize our lives. We realized this was going to be a long haul, and we would need to have some things brought from home. We also had to decide how to handle work and all the other activities our children were involved with. And, we knew we would have to stay connected with the scores of concerned people back home.

The nurses told us about a website where we could post what was happening so that family and friends could stay up-to-date. At first I didn't want to do that because I didn't want my attention to be anywhere but there in the hospital and on Isaiah. However, I changed my mind quickly when Stacey informed me that she had gotten a text from kids that Isaiah had died. I decided there would be no more misinformation! Randy and I started a Care Page for Isaiah.

Here is what was to become our first blog of many. . .

Posted July 27, 2008 at 9:52 p.m.

Well, where do I start? Isaiah is in an ICU unit in the Iowa City Children's Hospital with head trauma. Basically, he has some swelling and a blood clot on the brain. He may have C1 or C2 fractures in his neck. They just did some more tests with the results to be shared in the morning. The next few days will be critical for Isaiah, and he needs everyone's prayers. He is not conscious at this time by doctor's choice. Isaiah does have some cuts and broken bones around the right side of his face. Every other part of his body is healthy and strong. We have a lot of things we don't know about Isaiah's head injury. It is just a waiting game at this point, and it could be 2 to 4 days before we know more. What we do know is that God has got him. One of his favorite songs is Strong Tower by Kutless. It talks about when we are weak God is our strong tower, and He will never let us down. I told Isaiah that he needs to strap on those pads and put his game face on and go into battle, just a little different kind of battle, and he needs his team (that's us) to be by his side. They said the best patients are those who are physically strong, smart fighters. Those who know Isaiah know he is all three. We covet your prayers for Isaiah as well as for big brother Tony, sisters Kayla and Stacey, and Mom and Dad. Thank you for your support.

The next day. . .

Posted July 28, 2009 at 3:16 p.m.

Day two is upon us, and last night was a night of praying and little rest. Two of Isaiah's best friends were beside him until I kicked them out. I knew they needed their rest also. The pressure on the brain from the swelling is still of utmost concern. Again, the next 48 hours require patience and a lot of prayer. This morning the pressure was up, and he had a spike during the night that was of concern. The next move after evaluation this morning was to go back to surgery and put a tube in his head to help relieve the pressure. As of this writing, they have lowered his body temperature, and he is assisted with his breathing. One of the keys to his recovery is to keep him calm and still. As you players know, the only way to keep the "Beast" (football nickname) down is to put him down with some medication. Again, we know God has him, and I imagine God's arms wrapped around him as he rests. Keep praying for Cody and Jordan—-Cody as he faces surgery for his broken neck and Jordan for strength to support his two friends. I cannot express my heartfelt thanks for all the support we have had from friends and family these last two days. For those who are wondering about visiting Isaiah, they are letting people back in the PICU to look through the glass and at times to enter the room. Thanks for caring and listening. Randy

Those first few days we had a lot of time sitting around waiting, talking, and trying to piece together the events of the accident and what had happened to cause it. Jordan shared a little but was so upset and blaming himself that he just didn't want to talk about it much. The boys' coach and two of the other coaches came down to see Isaiah and Cody, to check on them and shared what they knew about the accident.

Coach said they were traveling from one field to another, and the three boys had jumped into Jordan's car. Jordan had driven that day because he had wrestling camp to go to and needed to leave the field early. Jordan was driving with Cody up front, and Isaiah had jumped in the back. Both boys up front had their seatbelts on, but Isaiah had not put one on since they were only traveling a few miles, and the law did not require it.

It was a dry time of year, so the dust on gravel roads was a problem. According to Cody, they were traveling at a speed of 50 miles per hour to keep up with the bus. Since it was dusty, it created a "white-out" effect on the road. Before they had gone very far, Isaiah screamed out, "BUS!" Jordan swerved to the left, but it was too late. The car rear-ended the stopped bus and proceeded to go under it.

The air bags went off, and Jordan was briefly knocked unconscious, while the roof of the car came down on Cody's neck. Isaiah's unrestrained body was propelled forward and hit the roof of the car as it came down upon impact, throwing him backwards into the back of the car.

Instantly, Isaiah was unconscious, and Cody could hear gurgling noises coming from him. Isaiah was choking on his own blood. Cody kept asking everyone how Isaiah was but did not get an answer. He was trapped under the car roof and could not do anything to help his friend. He could only listen with dread.

Thanks to the calmness and quick thinking of their coach and others with him, they held Isaiah's head and body and rolled him to his side so he would not choke on the blood. The paramedics arrived and took over Isaiah's care. They had a hard time finding a heartbeat and thought he was gone. After further checking, they were able to get a faint heart beat and administered a paralytic drug to keep him still as he was involuntarily moving his arms.

A life-flight helicopter was called and arrived to transport Isaiah to the nearest hospital. The paramedics had been working on him, and when he arrived at the hospital, the emergency room doctor decided he needed a bigger, more well-equipped hospital to care for his medical needs.

The coach was tearfully filled with grief for what had taken place that day and felt a sense of responsibility. But in reality, it was his presence of mind when it was most critical that helped save Isaiah's life. Though a young man himself, he showed great courage and quick response to something so terrible.

As they finished filling us in on the details it comforted me to know how the last hours before the accident had been for Isaiah. I wanted all the information I could get no matter how gruesome it was. I needed to know what had happened so someday I could tell Isaiah his story as I hoped for his recovery.

The second day was very difficult. Isaiah had to be unhooked from the machines and transported down for several CT scans, the surgery was done to place the catheter in his head, and an MRI was conducted to see if there were any fractures to his neck.

The nurse who took care of him that day was truly a Godsend for us. I just remember being in the room and asking all kinds of questions about his condition and what all the machines were for. She explained the situation to us in terms we could understand which Randy and I really appreciated.

We had shared with her how Isaiah was such a modest young man, and although he was "ripped" and ready to play football, he would never be seen without a shirt on, even when teased by his sisters. They would try to convince him to take off his shirt while mowing our yard so he could get a tan. He would not!

We left the room to talk with visitors who had come to see us, and when we returned, Isaiah had a gown on, covering his bare chest. I asked about the gown, and the nurse replied, "I heard you talking about how modest he was, and I didn't want him lying there feeling everyone was staring at his chest." This was just one of the many wonderful nurses who would be taking tender care of Isaiah.

The surgery to place the catheter in Isaiah's head went textbook perfect, and now the monitor could drain the spinal fluid to make room for his swelling brain. It frightened me to think they were removing spinal fluid from his body because to me, that meant it would affect his ability to walk, but they assured us that the body replaces this fluid on a regular basis. Dr. Jackson also informed us that Isaiah had an Intracerebral Hemorrhage, a clot deep in the middle of his brain which they could not remove without risking extensive damage.

He described Isaiah's injury as a diffuse axonal injury. This meant the pathways that connect the different areas of the brain had been damaged. We would later find out that was the reason Isaiah hadn't had a bone flap, where a section of the skull is removed to relieve pressure in a certain area of the skull. His brain was swelling all over. They would have had to remove his entire skull!

He was put on a cooling blanket to keep his body temperature down and was intubated which meant a machine was breathing for him since he couldn't breathe on his own. He was placed on a drug called Remifentinil for pain, but the only problem was they couldn't leave him on one particular pain medication or his body could become addicted, so they periodically switched his pain meds.

Then came a day I will never forget. We were in the room when they decided to "bring him out" of the medically induced coma. I guess I didn't know exactly what to expect. I only knew I needed to be there no matter what because what if Isaiah could hear us or opened his eyes? I wanted to be there to reassure him. As soon as they brought him out, his body started to tremor (neuro-storming) and he started "posturing." This was caused from the shock to his body, and it caused him to straighten his arms and then rotate them in an inward direction toward his body.

It scared me so much, but I couldn't let on. I wanted him to know I was there in case he could hear me. All I could say in those split seconds was that I loved him and that God was with him. Then they quickly put him back into the coma, and his body relaxed again.

Since Isaiah was unable to breathe on his own or use any of his bodily functions, a nasogastric tube was placed in his nose to feed him, and a urinary catheter was inserted into his bladder.

To prevent blood clots from forming in his legs and to help with circulation, anti-embolism stockings were placed on both his legs. They had little machines that would alternate expanding and contracting to keep blood flowing to his feet. The nurses also repositioned his body every so often to keep him from getting bed sores.

The second day was coming to an end, and so far Isaiah was hanging onto life. We knew many, many people were praying for him. Outside the hospital is a healing garden. It has a peaceful little fountain that runs into a small stream meandering around a beautifully landscaped garden. It was dark, and this was a place of solace for Randy that night. As he sat out there praying, asking God for strength and direction, he said God's quiet voice spoke to his mind and said, "I know what you are going through. I gave my son, a ransom for many. I understand, and I will walk with you. Just trust in Me."

He shared this with me when he came back up to Isaiah's room. I told him that God had also given me comfort in the verses from Isaiah 40: 28-31: *"Do you not know? Have you not heard? The Lord is the everlasting God, the Creator of the ends of the earth. He will not grow tired or weary, and his understanding no one can fathom. He gives strength to the weary, and increases the power of the weak. Even youths grow tired and weary, young men stumble and fall; but those who hope in the Lord will renew their strength. They will soar on wings like eagles; they WILL RUN and not grow weary; they WILL WALK and not be faint."*

The words WILL RUN and WILL WALK struck me. What was God trying to tell me? Was Isaiah going to walk again? Would he even be able to run? How little faith we have at times, but this was such a clear message to me that I quickly wrote it down and placed it on the glass window outside Isaiah's room. I needed that daily reminder of His promise, and I would cling to it every day, no matter what the doctors said, for nothing is impossible with God!

Randy and I prayed together in Isaiah's room. After sharing what God had spoken to each of us separately, we decided right there that no matter what happened, we would give God all the glory and praise Him in this storm. If Isaiah lived, we would praise Him; if he decided to take Isaiah to Heaven, we would praise Him. After all, why should we be spared from heartache? We deserved punishment for the sins we've committed against Him, and yet He had given us so much. Isaiah was in His hands now.

By late evening of the third day, Dr. Jackson came into Isaiah's room and said the MRI had shown there were no fractures in Isaiah's neck, so the neck collar came off. Praise God from whom all blessings flow! It was amazing how quickly songs were the first things to pop into my head when we received any kind of news. This would be the new normal for me in the weeks to follow. God would bring a song to my mind, I would sing it to myself, and it would bring me peace.

We were not out of the critical period yet, but we were comforted in knowing we were not alone and neither was Isaiah. Just as Isaiah's name means *salvation of the LORD*, his "salvation" from this world would come from the One who created him. God had blessed us with him, Tony, Kayla, and Stacey. As we kept vigil at his bedside that night, I remembered happier times together as a family.

Chapter Three
Growing Up Years

*G*rowing up in rural Iowa is a wonderful experience for young children. During our children's earliest years, we lived on a farm near Buffalo Center. Randy farmed the ground around our place and far-rowed and raised hogs for market. We also had a couple hundred head of feeder cattle. This meant there were chores every day that included feeding and bedding the animals, giving shots to the little piglets, and cleaning out stalls.

It instilled in our children a good work ethic that has carried through to their jobs today. They had chores they were responsible for, and we were pleased at how well they handled those responsibilities. As with any acreage, there is always lots of mowing to be done as well, so besides Randy and me, Tony and Kayla would also take turns running the mower. It wasn't like it was hard work. It was more fun for them since we had a zero-turn mower that allowed them to run at a faster speed and spin around any trees or shrubs with a tight turn.

While Randy worked out in the fields and with the livestock, I was able to be home with our four children. Growing up, I loved kids, and it was my dream to be at home with my own children as they grew up. When the time came for Tony to begin school, I was having a difficult time thinking of him going away for a better part of the day. Randy and I talked about what options we had and decided to send him to a private Christian school about twenty-five minutes away.

It was important to us that our children have a Christian upbringing. The Christian school provided that for Tony and Kayla for a couple years but in the summer before Kayla was to start first grade and Tony third grade, we talked about home schooling them. This concept was new to me, but I wanted to try it so I could keep my children close to me at home and also instill biblical values in them. The drive to the Christian school was becoming more difficult having to take all four children along, and the tuition was expensive.

So the summer of 1994 began our adventure into home schooling our children. Our day began with the pledges and a Bible study. We would study geography and history together, but they did math and language at their individual levels. It was a bit more laid back than the usual rushing out the door to get to school and always being on the road, and it provided time for all four of them to play together during the afternoons.

During the eleven years that we homeschooled, Tony, Kayla, Isaiah, and Stacey bonded and enjoyed many hours together, from building forts out of the straw up in the haymow to driving the go-cart around and around the grove. Of course, as with many farms, we had lots of cats and a dog. At one time we had as many as 30 cats and went through a tremendous amount of cat food!

In the spring when the mother cats were having their kittens, Tony and Kayla would climb up into the haymow and search for holes in the straw to try and find the kittens. It was like Christmas because we never knew what color the kittens would be or how many we would find. With all this attention, our kittens were never wild but very tame and would hang around the back door until the kids came out to play.

As Tony and Kayla grew, they ventured farther out and walked the quarter mile across our field to the creek. They were always planning these excursions and even engineered a rope bridge to get them from one side of the creek to the other. There were several trees along the creek, so it made for a great hide out! When friends came over, they would take them out there and play for hours.

This creek was also deep enough for Tony and Kayla to float down it using either old tire tubes or a raft they had built. I would drop them off at one bridge and pick them up at the next bridge a mile away. These trips led to many wonderful memories. One time as they floated along, a doe and her two fawns were standing in the creek getting a drink. When the doe saw the kids, she made a snorting sound and stomped her front leg as a warning to the fawns to run. One obeyed quickly, but the other stayed longer, and Tony and Kayla were able to float up close to the fawn before it bolted off with the others.

On another journey on the creek, they spotted a large, prehistoric-looking snapping turtle moving up the side of the bank. It was large enough to send both of them scrambling up the bank, leaving shoes behind, and running bare foot straight home across the field. Their eyes were still as big as saucers as they told me of their adventure!

In the back of our acreage was a pole building. Three sides were solid with tin closing them in, and on the open east side were poles that held up the building. Pigeons liked to roost on the overhang, and, on occasion, so did screech owls.

Stacey, the youngest of the four, didn't always get to go out on all the creek excursions with the older three. But when they stayed on the yard, she was able to play with her siblings. On this particular day, they all were playing in the pole barn when they heard a screeching sound. There, perched in the overhang, were two screech owls.

The older three kids were so excited to see them that they ran to the house to get me. In all their excitement, they forgot about Stacey. By then, she was terrified that these owls with the large, yellow eyes would swoop down and grab her, so she hid under a wagon, hoping help would come before she was taken! She was relieved when we all returned, and I tried to comfort her with the knowledge that they were so small that they could never carry her and were probably just as afraid of her as she was of them.

Many farm places have groves of trees around them to help protect from the cold winds that blow across the fields in the wintertime. The trees help to keep the snow from piling up in the yard as well. Children always delight in climbing their branches and our four were no different.

They loved climbing our trees. In fact, they each claimed their own special tree.

I remember the day very clearly when my children decided to test the strength of my heart! I was in fixing lunch for them, and they were out playing in the trees. Stacey happened to fall and land on some partially buried barbed wire. It made a small puncture wound on her forehead. Tony decided they needed to play a trick on me, so they squeezed the wound so a small drop of blood came from the opening. Then he picked her up and told her not to move.

I looked out the window to see where they were before calling them in. I remember seeing Kayla and Isaiah, their heads down, walking alongside Tony, who was carrying Stacey. She wasn't moving, and my heart dropped. I ran out to them and asked what had happened.

Tony explained the circumstances of the fall and how Stacey hadn't moved. I took her from him and scrutinized her forehead. As I examined her, a smile broke across her face. I was torn between two emotions... relief and anger! After a few wise words to them all about the little boy who cried wolf, we proceeded into the house to eat our meal.

Later that same day, Randy's mom stopped out to visit, and while we sat outside, the kids played in their favorite trees. Isaiah slipped while climbing down his tree and ran a sliver up his bare leg. He came hobbling across the yard with Tony, Kayla, and Stacey beside him to help him walk.

Naturally, my first thought was, "Oh, no! They are now going to try and pretend that Isaiah is really hurt." But as he got closer, I could see something deep inside his lower leg. We ended up in the emergency room to have it removed, and he ended up with a few stitches in his leg.

My children spent many hours playing together and became very close. I have never regretted the time home schooling them. The older siblings helped out with the younger ones, and they stuck up for each other if other kids picked on one of them.

We were fortunate to have a local church that offered the Awana Club for our youth. It is a club that starts when children are four-to-five years old. They receive a vest and a book filled with Bible verses to memorize and community service projects to complete before they can move on to the next book. They earn awards after finishing each book. My four enjoyed this since many of their friends attended Awana too. Randy and I figured out that by the time they were done with the Awana program, they had, at the very least, memorized over 900 Bible verses.

We have so many great memories of our time on the acreage near Buffalo Center, but in 2000, Randy took a new job in Allison, which meant we would have to move. There were many tears shed as we left dear friends, but we felt God was moving us to be closer to my family, and so we went.

Our girls were attached to the cats and wanted to bring them all with us, but we explained that we just couldn't take them all. We chose to bring four along and that was it. But about the time we were going to move, Cheyenne, a mother cat, was very much ready to give birth, and we didn't want her alone at the farm to have the kittens, so Cheyenne got to join us as well.

It was mid-July when we made the trip, packing all our belongings into two separate vehicles. Randy and the boys were in one, and I was with the girls along with the cats in their pet carriers. Of course, this would be the time, in 95-degree heat, that Cheyenne went into labor, right there in the back of the van!

Kayla kept us informed about Cheyenne's condition as we traveled down the highway. At one point, the cat was panting so bad that we had to stop and try to get her to drink a little bit of water. One kitten, then two, and by the time we reached our new rural home, Cheyenne had been blessed with seven kittens! So much for only taking a few!

At the time of the move, Tony and Kayla entered public school for the first time: Tony as a freshman, and Kayla as a seventh grader. Tony and Kayla adjusted to school and loved it. They were involved in sports and were thriving. Isaiah and Stacey enjoyed the extra time with Mom. When I look back on it now, I realize how this time was important for me to help the two younger ones see how God works in everyday life.

We were blessed to be able to put together a puppet show for the elementary students at Allison-Bristow School. Isaiah and Stacey helped me come up with a story that taught a lesson. Next, we created a skit in which we could use our puppets and then built background scenery to fit the story. This became an annual event for about four years.

Even though things had changed, and we were not all home every day, the kids were close to each other. It was fun to watch them outside enjoying activities together. Although there are six years between Tony and Isaiah, Isaiah had grown to the point he was just as tall as Tony, and they started doing more things together like pheasant hunting and deer hunting.

Pheasant hunting became the annual thing to do the first weekend in November. Randy would take Tony and Isaiah back up to Buffalo Center. They stayed at Grandma's and then walked for miles looking for pheasants. When noon came, they traveled back to her house and sat down for what looked like a Thanksgiving feast. Grandmas love it when you walk away from the table moaning and groaning because you ate so much of their good food!

When Isaiah turned fifteen, he wanted to purchase a motorcycle since Randy and Tony already had their own. He had detasseled that summer and saved his money to buy a motorcycle from a friend of ours. Now we had our own motorcycle gang! They loved going for cruises around the area and spending that time together.

Randy and I went to all the football games in the fall to watch Isaiah plow over or tackle anyone who got in his way. He was an intense player and loved the game. I almost felt sorry for anyone who had to be across from him! He was not the biggest kid out on the field but he made up for that with the intensity he brought.

Stacey enjoyed playing basketball and learning all there was to know about her favorite sport. By now, she and Isaiah were both in public school. They loved it and enjoyed getting to know all the new kids at school.

Our lives were not so much different from other Iowa families, and Randy and I delighted in watching our children grow and mature. Everything seemed to be going along fine, with very few troubles to speak of considering we had such active children. I was blessed to see them love each other and want to be in each other's company. Life was good! So many great memories...

Chapter Four
First Seventy-Two Hours

*I*t was Day 3, and many wonderful visitors had come to see Isaiah and offer us prayer as well as food to eat while we were there. We gratefully accepted all the granola bars, quick oatmeal for breakfast, water bottles, and many other thoughtful gifts. It saved us from having to eat at the cafeteria every day, and we also had so much that we were able to share with the doctors and nurses in the PICU.

Pastor Mike and Linda Nemmers came by that Tuesday morning. They had been instrumental in leading Randy and me to a personal relationship with Jesus during a home Bible study many years before, and now they came to pray with us and encourage us.

As Mike prayed over Isaiah, he made the comment that this had not come as a surprise to God. He knew this was going to happen to Isaiah. He prayed for courage and peace and comfort for us and complete healing for Isaiah.

Not a surprise to God is what leaped out at me. That was right! This was known by God all along. He knew it was going to happen and exactly how it was going to turn out. Although Randy and I did not know, I took comfort in being reminded of this and even more confident in what I had believed would happen: Isaiah would Walk and Run again!

I usually would not be called an optimist. As a mother, I worried about my children and prayed they would grow up to be healthy, wise adults who loved the Lord and followed Him. I worried when they were late getting home from ball games or from a date. But for some reason, this time I was confident that God was going to keep this promise. No one could convince me otherwise, even though we had well-meaning relatives that offered us no encouragement that Isaiah would ever be normal again.

Less than a half hour after their visit, we began to see just how God would use our circumstances there in Iowa City and perhaps in many other places that we will never know. I had posted pictures of Isaiah along with the verses from Isaiah 40 on his window, and one of the other women, whose grandson was a patient in the same ward because of a car accident, came up to me and asked to speak to me.

She said she had read the verses and was so struck by them that she wanted to know more about the Bible and God and where our strength came from. It had been a very long time since she had attended church. She was in great need of something bigger than herself to hold onto as they faced a similar situation, a grandson with a traumatic brain injury.

I told her she could purchase a Bible at the book store in the hospital, and Pastor Mike told us to give her the verse from *Jeremiah 29:11*: *I know the plans I have for you, declares the Lord, plans to give you a hope and a future.* Relieved, she went directly down to buy her Bible and began reading it to her grandson, who was also still unconscious. It was amazing to see her own faith grow and to witness the peace she received from reading the Bible.

God was working even through our terrible circumstances, and I felt so humbled to be used by Him and to be comforted as I was comforting others. It's hard to explain, but it seemed the more I reached out to comfort other families, the more I experienced peace myself. Although I would never want to go through something like this ever again, I would not trade the closeness to Jesus I was experiencing and how real He was to me.

Ranae D. Krull

Posted July 29, 2008 at 6:35 a.m.

This is the day the Lord has made. We will rejoice and be glad in it. We cannot thank you enough for all your precious prayers going up for Isaiah, Cody, and Jordan. We can definitely feel God's hand on all of us and see Him working, not only physically, but also mentally and emotionally. What a mighty God we serve!

We are still waiting to hear the results of the MRI Isaiah had last night, but we talked to his nurse this morning after the neuro-surgeons made their rounds. She said they were taking him briefly off his meds to see what kind of response they get from him when they touch him. We are praying he will respond by reaching for the area they are touching. This would be wonderful as it would show them what he is capable of responding to at this time. All his vitals are good, and his swelling is staying at a level they like to see at this point after his accident. He is responding a bit when they take off his wrappings, or if they check his pupil dilation, the nurse said he stiffens and tries to fight it. What else could we expect from a fighter?

We will continue to covet your prayers in the recovery process not only for Isaiah, but for Cody and Jordan as well. At times like these, you are all a great support to our families, and we cannot express enough how grateful and thankful we are to each of you. We are praying for a full recovery for Isaiah, and we know our GOD is MIGHTY TO SAVE even beyond the salvation of our souls to the healing of our bodies. He did raise a dead man, so we know this is simple for Him! Thank you so much...

For the first week in PICU, we set up camp in the family lounge down the hall from Isaiah's room. We slept on the couches and chairs, which weren't the most comfortable, but it was a place to lie down. We took turns staying in Isaiah's room at night. We just wanted to be close so we'd be there if something should happen.

The care pages became a source of encouragement for our family. Randy and I were the ones who posted most about what was going on with Isaiah, but every once in a while, Stacey or Kayla would post something on there as well. The words from so many would come back, and it was so encouraging to read verses from Scripture or words from a song that would hit us right where we needed it at the time.

Our youngest daughter, Stacey, decided to write the following blog on the fifth day after the accident. She was 15 at the time and about to enter the ninth grade that fall.

Posted July 31, 2008 at 1:29 a.m.

Hey, everyone, this is Stacey. I thought I would write on here. Since this has been helping my parents, it should help me. I don't have any new updates on Ike's condition or anything. I just thought I'd write down how I'm feeling at this point.

Where should I begin? There are so many things that are going through my mind right now. It's very overwhelming. I'm sitting next to Ike, and I so badly want him to wake up and look at me. I want this nightmare to end. It's really tough seeing your best friend lying there, but I know God has a reason for everything.

I'm already starting to learn from all of this. We never know how much time we have on this earth, and we can never take back a day we've lived. I have always said, "Live your life to the fullest." I thought I was, always staying positive about life and just living. I was so wrong. I don't live life to the fullest.

Here all I've been thinking about lately is myself and how I want to fit in when school starts up. How I want to be with the so-called "cool" crowd. Life isn't about trying to fit in with other people. It's about being true to yourself and what you believe in. Isaiah is a perfect example of a person who lives out his faith and doesn't care what others think of him. He has his best friends, his family, and his God. What else could he need? When I think about Ike, I just want to be like him. I want to stand up for my faith. I don't know if I'll be in a car accident tomorrow or if I will have a heart attack. I do know now that every day I have to show the ones I love that I love them. I have to stand up for Jesus every day. I've got to admit that it is very hard for me to show emotions or show people I really do care about them, but through this, I'm learning to open up more to the ones I love and to the ones who care about me.

I just really want my brother back right now. I want him to pick me up and throw me over his shoulders like he used to. I even want him to call me a "turd cutter," which he had been calling me lately. But most of all, I just need God to fill in my emptiness. I need Him to be my strong tower and to fully rely on Him. If anyone can heal Isaiah completely and make him stronger than before, that's God. Right now I'm holding onto His plan for this whole thing. Even though at times this does suck really bad, God is doing something here…

Posted July 31, 2008, at 6:28 p.m. by Randy

Okay, I'm going to try this again. Last night I did try to post a new message by using the laptop in Isaiah's room, and as I was finishing up, the computer timed me out just as I pushed the post tab. Unbelievable! But then it hit me that last night's posting was kind of a tough one, so the Lord just didn't want that one going out of the room.

Thank you for all the support today. It has been overwhelming to be loved by so many people. Just to see the impact that Isaiah has had on so many people.

The numbers on the screens were good all throughout the night and day. He had his first real neurological exam to develop a baseline to measure his recovery. That was very difficult to watch because when they brought him partially out of his medical coma, he started to shake and tremble. They then started going through the exam, and some was good as we would hope, and others showed no response at this time. This will give them a baseline for improvements.

His heart beat increases along with his blood pressure when they bring him out. The exciting thing is that he initiates taking his own breaths and at a more rapid pace than what the machine is producing.

He is lying there quietly this evening, and we wait patiently for the next day. Through this whole event in our lives, God is touching hearts, and I pray that all our hearts may be changed to love others and to seek our Heavenly Father. Some have said, "Your family is so religious." I would like you to understand it is not being religious but having a relationship with Jesus Christ that is the difference. The peace comes from knowing God is in control no matter what happens. God loves all of us, but because of sin in this world, there are sorrows and trials. We don't have to walk it alone. We have Jesus to hold onto, and He uses others to help us as we walk. I am so proud of my kids and how they are handling this stage in their lives.

Be strong, Isaiah. You have a lot of people praying and loving you and your family.

Isaiah had a very special visit today by his best friend, Cody. Yes, when Cody spoke to Isaiah, his heart rate went up, and Isaiah had some slight hand squeezing going on. This is where I stop with this one because I'm thinking of Mike. Love you. Jordan was standing right there across the bed from Cody.

I think I'm going to end here before I get timed out again.

Posted July 31, 2008 at 11:20 p.m. by Kayla

I'm not very good at putting the feelings in my heart into words. But when I got into my car today to head home from work, I was feeling kind of down, not wanting to leave my little brother there…there was just this ache in my heart. But God, being the awesome God that He is, lifted up my spirit with this song. I became a Christian my senior year of high school because of this group, Casting Crowns, and God used them again to tell me that He's still here…loving me and my family, and that He's taking care of my little brother when I doubt His presence. I love you, Isaiah!!

> *Chorus:*
> *And I'll praise you in this storm,*
> *And I will lift my hands,*
> *For You are who You are*
> *No matter where I am.*
> *And every tear I cry,*
> *You hold in Your hand.*
> *You never left my side,*
> *And though my heart is torn,*
> *I will praise You in this storm.*

When I got onto the care pages and read the messages the girls had written, I was so encouraged to find them leaning on the Lord. Even though they could not understand why this happened to their brother, they were seeing God use it in the lives of others. Here were two young women experiencing something so painful, and yet they realized God was at work and doing something through this. God is always present, and He spared Isaiah for a reason. We all knew he shouldn't be alive, and yet he was and was fighting for all he was worth.

After spending a week living in the family lounge, we finally got a room right in the hospital. They had a section on another floor where anyone with children as patients could stay at a reduced rate. They were made-over hospital rooms that reminded me of a hotel room. It was so nice to be able to actually sleep in a bed. It was very difficult the first few nights to stay in the room because in my heart I felt I needed to be up with Isaiah. But Randy was wise in making me get a good night's rest. Although I felt an inexplicable peace, I knew I needed to keep up my strength in order to do what I had to do to take care of Isaiah.

The days seemed to blend together, and I couldn't have told anyone what day of the week it was or how long we had been in the hospital. It was getting to the point that I missed hearing Isaiah's voice so badly, and I was trying to think of what I could do to hear him again. The thought of calling his cell phone to listen to his voice mail message dawned on me. So I did. Not just once, but several times. It was wonderful hearing the same voice saying, "Hey, this is Isaiah. Can't come to the phone now, but leave a message, and I'll get back to you as soon as I can." Kayla and Stacey had been feeling the same way, so they had been accessing his voice mail too. Unfortunately, I didn't realize that once a person's voice mail is full, it won't let people hear the message anymore. Isaiah had a lock on his phone, so we were unable to get in and erase all the voice mails. I could only pray that the next time I'd hear his voice, it would be from his own lips.

By Thursday, we had gotten to know many of the nurses, and they were wonderful. We'd be in the room at one in the morning, and the nurse watching over Isaiah would help us understand some of the things going on with him. They'd take time to explain what all the numbers on the monitors meant and would also decipher all the medical terms the doctors used into words we could understand.

Randy has always been one who likes to joke around. One particular evening, as we were bringing a midnight snack to the nurses on duty, Randy began joking with them about how many cute nurses there were and how young they all seemed to be. He informed them that we had an older son, Tony, who was single and without a girlfriend. It didn't take long for one of the nurses to reply with, "Which nurses are you referring to?" This nurse declared that Bailey was one of those young nurses and was very sweet and indeed quite available!

Bailey had taken such great care of Isaiah, and she was the nurse who had covered his bare chest when she found out he was modest. We also realized she was the one who had given Randy and me the Tylenol the very first night we were there.

Randy and I told the nurses that Tony would be sleeping in Isaiah's room that night, so they could "check him out" to make sure he met their standards for one of their nurses. They all laughed, and we didn't expect anything to come of it.

Tony, Kayla, Stacey, and Jordan were hanging out in the family lounge playing UNO, trying to pass the time. Randy told them it was time to get some rest and that Tony needed to head down to Isaiah's room. He reminded Tony to make sure to check in with the nurses to let them know he was the brother and to ask if it would be okay for him to sleep in the room.

As Tony approached the nurses' station and made sure they knew he was Isaiah's brother, they all smiled and nodded their heads rather sheepishly. Tony momentarily felt a little strange but then didn't give it another thought. He went in and stood over Isaiah, talking to him and holding his hand.

One of the nurses came in to "check" on Isaiah and began asking Tony a number of questions about himself. Now he was getting the picture! She handed him a note and said Bailey would not object to having him call her. He simply smiled and placed the note in his pocket. It would be a few days before he felt like he could call her, but he had noticed her as well and was thankful to receive the number.

We never know when we are in the middle of a storm what God has planned, but a serious relationship would develop between Tony and Bailey. She never took care of Isaiah again while we were in the PICU, but she was around there working, so we all got to know her and came to love her.

How can we not help but love and adore a God who, in the midst of trials, brings these little glimmers of hope? In these instances, He knows what we're going through, and He is there every step of the way.

2 Corinthians 4:16-18: "Therefore we do not lose heart. Though outwardly we are wasting away, yet inwardly we are being renewed day by day. For our light and momentary troubles are achieving for us an eternal glory that far outweighs them all. So we fix our eyes not on what we see, but on what is unseen. For what is seen is temporary, but what is unseen is eternal."

These were verses that Randy had read earlier in the week, and as God was healing Isaiah, His words were healing us.

Posted August 2, 2008 by Ranae

Good morning to all our precious supporters!!! We cannot thank you enough for all the support we are receiving, either by visitors or calls or prayers or the great messages on this page. Just an update: Isaiah was running a fever last night, about 101 degrees. They are checking on a possible pneumonia, which is common when a person is on a ventilator. They were already on top of it with antibiotics, and they gave him another round just to make sure he was covered. By this morning his temperature was back to normal. Praise God! Isaiah is resting, and all his numbers are good.

It was great to see the coaches come to see him. I'm hoping they can go back to the team and encourage them on how well Isaiah is doing and encourage them to take their training seriously, because being physically fit is one thing Isaiah has going for him right now.

I have to admit that I woke up this morning with a fear of the "what if's?" Right away the Lord put on my heart the verse from Isaiah 38: "…only the living can praise You." We have an enemy that seeks to destroy us either by tempting us to sin or by getting us down and causing us to fear. One thing our Isaiah has always said is NO FEAR! These are the times we need to take charge and fight back, using the most powerful weapon known to man. No, it's not the nuke! It's the Word of God. The Bible says that when our enemy comes, we need to use God's Word to ward him off because he has to obey God's command. Pretty powerful!

Stacey and Randy are down at the field house lifting weights and shooting some hoops. Good therapy! Tony and Kayla are back home fulfilling their work duties, even though they would love to be here. So pray for them to be strong because I know they all want to be here should Isaiah open his eyes.

Chapter Five
So Many Decisions

Posted August 3, 2008 at 11:43 a.m. by Ranae

Breathe in, breathe out. It seems we take these breaths for granted, but for Isaiah this is big. Today they are going to increase the time he is off the vent, and he has been doing really well with this. He has also been coughing some good coughs that bring up junk from his lungs, which helps to keep them clean. They did an EKG during the night to check on some irregular heart beats, but that all came back fine. Right now they are hooking him up to an EEG to get a baseline on his brain activity. These are all standard procedures for this type of injury. Oh, my goodness! I'm starting to sound like a nurse! Scary!

I miss being at church this morning, and I will have to admit I am struggling a bit because it has been a week today that we got the news, and I find myself missing Isaiah--his hugs, his talking about what went on at detasseling, the new speakers he put into his car. You know, everyone keeps saying, "We just can't believe how well you are doing. You are so strong." It's not true!! God is the strong One, and we are all leaning on Him. I believe God has put on my heart and on Randy's that Isaiah is going to come through this 100%, and we are hanging onto that promise. Romans 4:20-21: "Yet he did not waver through unbelief regarding the promise of God, but was strengthened in his faith and gave glory to God, being fully persuaded that God had power to do what He promised."

36

I've gone along in my faith and always thought I was a pretty strong believer, but God has been working to further strengthen my faith this entire week. I keep thinking about a message our pastor had a few weeks back about what we really deserve from God, and it is punishment for the sins we've committed against Him. And yet, while we were yet sinners, Christ died for us. The payment we deserve is death, a separation from God, but the gift He has given us is eternal life. Isaiah has believed this, and I can't help but think that even in his sedated state, GOD is speaking to him and guiding him through this all.

*E*ach day brought new challenges but also a renewed hope that Isaiah was slowly recovering. He was hooked up to all kinds of wires that monitored his condition, and there were just so many unknowns and issues to deal with. Was there much brain activity, or was something else going on? I hadn't even thought of the possibility that there could be little brain activity or that he could be having seizures.

Posted August 4, 2008 by Ranae

Luke 1:17: "For NOTHING is impossible with GOD!" I just came from Isaiah's room, and I'm shaking because I'm overwhelmed by the power of prayer for Isaiah and his recovery! The doctors were making their rounds, so I listened in on what they were saying (like I can understand it anyway). But I did understand that he is doing an excellent job on his breathing (He's gone the last 2 hours on his own!) and that his ICP has stayed under 10. They backed off the amount of spinal fluid they were taking out to see how his body would compensate, and his number only went up to 11.

They decided to bring him out of his sedation to see how the ICP would respond. It remained at 11–12 and only spiked briefly to 15. His heart rate increased to about 129 beats per minute but then came back below 100. I know these numbers might be confusing for some, but I'm learning these were all good signs that he was tolerating all of it!

Then I asked Isaiah to wiggle his toes, and HE DID! Twice! He squeezed the nurse's hand with his left hand and also with his right. He was also blinking his eyes. Since he did so well with all of this, they are talking about doing the surgery on his cheek today or tomorrow, whenever they can get him into OR.

I can't tell you how elated I am. I'm shaking as I'm typing this because I want to fall on my knees and say to God, "I'm so sorry I ever had doubts!"

Thank you all for praying. I'm keeping a journal of all of this so when Isaiah recovers, he will be able to share his story and praise his Mighty Maker and reach even more people to follow the GOD he loves!

Oh, I just thought about the EEG he had yesterday. That came back fine, no seizures going on in his head!! Yet another Praise!!

Posted August 4, 2008 by Randy

Being 100 miles away and not seeing those first purposeful movements was tough. It is interesting. You think at times when something happens like this to your family that the world stops. NOT, as the kids would say. We do know that Isaiah's accident has disrupted many lives, and people are praying and caring and that is so evident, but there is still an aspect of life that goes on called work and responsibility.

It was exciting to get that phone call from Ranae and cry a bit before going back to my meeting. Stacey seems to be doing okay at the basketball camp. She texted me to see if I could drop off some Twizzlers when I came to watch her game tonight. They have teams put together, and people can watch in the evenings. Since the camp is at Wartburg in Waverly, that is not a problem. So I will be watching basketball later.

Oh, by the way, this is not an Isaiah update. Sorry. It is Randy sharing life. Yes, I did my breakfast dishes this morning and even attempted to make the bed. And, Michael, I want you to know the dog finally got over it and let me pet her this morning. Licorice has been protesting since we have been gone and goes right to Michael, her dog sitter, over me. Traitor!

Anyway, keep praying for a full recovery for Isaiah. God is being glorified even through this accident.

Randy was back at work, trying to keep things going on at home. Stacey had gone to a basketball camp for a few days. Kayla returned to work and was preparing for college classes to begin. Tony had just been hired by the Waverly Police Department and faced having to be a couple hours away for training for up to 12 weeks.

They all took turns coming down to Iowa City and staying with me. It was lonely at times without them. There were a few times I remember breaking down. I'd wake up early so I could get up to Isaiah's room before the doctors made their rounds. I would stand in the shower and found this a safe place for me to cry, asking God the questions… *WHY? Why Isaiah? Give me strength to face yet another day! Help me to see what You are doing here and to continue to trust You.* As quickly as I felt overwhelmed, I would dry my tears and feel renewed. God was so faithful. How could I not help but love Him all the more?

Life was still moving forward, and I hadn't left the hospital in almost three weeks. School was approaching, and Stacey needed some school supplies and clothes. When she and Randy came down that weekend, Randy suggested I go with her to the local mall and shop and get out for a bit. I was torn about leaving the hospital, but I knew I needed to spend time with Stacey before she started high school without me there.

It was the strangest feeling to drive to the mall and then sit outside a dressing room. People were laughing, and some teens were joking around not far from where I was sitting. How could they act as if nothing was wrong? My son lay in a hospital room fighting for his life, and they were laughing. It just bothered me. I called Randy and told him how difficult it was. He knew exactly how I was feeling because he had been going through that same struggle at home. Life does go on, and we had to realize that it would for us too. It would just be different from now on.

The doctors began to clamp off Isaiah's vent to see if he could handle breathing on his own. Little by little he was going two hours, then four hours, and then overnight, breathing on his own. By Day 10, they decided he was doing well enough to completely remove the vent—not something I could watch. I stood outside the door, and I could hear him gasp. That was too much for me to see. My dear sister was there with me, and my sister-in-law watched from inside the room. Her words to me were, "Isaiah is such a tough kid. I will never get over how tough he is."

Back home many people were still struggling through their losses because of June's serious flooding. Samaritan's Purse had arrived with a team of rapid-relief counselors. A couple who had heard about Isaiah's accident decided to come down to Iowa City and pray with Randy and me and see Isaiah. Ken and Marilyn had posted a prayer chain for Isaiah on the Billy Graham World Wide Prayer Chain. When they shared this news with us, I was overcome with emotion. Words cannot express how overjoyed and humbled we felt to know that so many people were praying for Isaiah, people who would never meet him. Ken and Marilyn stayed and visited with us for awhile and came into Isaiah's room to pray over him.

About a week after their visit, we had one of those very difficult days because we had to make a decision about where Isaiah would be going for his inpatient rehabilitation. We had no clue where that should be or what kind of care he was going to need. Then we noticed a gentleman walking toward us in the hall just down from Isaiah's room. Ron Dennis, an older man from Samaritan's Purse, asked if we were Isaiah's parents. He said he had spoken with a young youth leader at our church who had worked with Isaiah. This youth leader had shared how impressed he always was at how much Isaiah knew about the Bible and how strong he was in his faith. Mr. Dennis wanted to "meet" this young man and pray over him before he caught a flight to his home.

We never turned down anyone who would pray for Isaiah, so we took him to the room. Never before had I heard someone pray with such confidence in God and His healing power. I have to admit, I did peek a few times at Isaiah. I was so uplifted by this heartfelt prayer that I was expecting Isaiah to rise up at that very moment and ask what was going on! It was very powerful for us, and it came at just the time we needed it.

Posted August 6, 2008 by Ranae

"I said, 'Oh, that I had the wings of a dove! I would fly away and be at rest--I would flee far away and stay in the desert; I would hurry to my place of shelter, far from the tempest and storm.'" Psalms 55:6-8. That was what I felt when we got the call that Isaiah had been in an accident: "God, just let me run away to a safe place where none of this is real."

That was 1 ½ weeks ago. The rest of the verses in Psalms 55:16-17 say, "But I call to God, and the Lord saves me. Evening, morning and noon I called to You for help. I will lie down and sleep in peace, for You alone, O Lord, make me dwell in safety."

Now I am seeing what it is that God is wanting to teach me through all of this. There are those out there who don't know who He is and His great desire that all men come to know Him. It's more than just a head knowledge. It's with the heart. Personal! I think, "God, I don't want to walk this path...I can't do it." But then in His quiet, gentle voice He says, "I'm with you. I want you to be a light to those who are around you."

I feel so unworthy for Him to use me, but each day He puts precious people in our midst: the wonderful nurses, the doctors who are His hands, the others affected by some sort of tragedy. I'm not a strong person, but God is upholding each of us, and we know He will accomplish what He desires and that is always the best!

I can't believe it, but they took Isaiah off the catheter this morning, and this afternoon his breathing tube came out! He has been coughing a lot to try to get the gunk (my medical term) out of his lungs. His heart rate is a little fast, but right now it has come down, and he's resting peacefully.

If he gets along okay tomorrow, he will have surgery on his cheek on Friday morning. This will be quite a procedure.

Some of the varsity football players showed up this morning, and what a treat to see those strapping young men! What a lift not only for us but Cody as well. Thanks, guys, for your support! What a great group!

Over the next few days, we heard from people who were trying to help us make the tough decisions about where Isaiah would spend his initial rehab. The wonderful doctor who came on duty Day 13 was a game changer! Isaiah's recovery now involved rapid changes, and this doctor spoke to us in terms we could understand. He also encouraged the residents and fellows to address us similarly as they made their rounds. He told them to let us know if the numbers they rattled off were improvements from the day before.

At this point, Isaiah was off the ventilator, and they had taken out the catheter from his head. Pneumonia had set in, and his skilled respiratory therapists were wonderful at keeping him suctioned out when he coughed up phlegm from his lungs. They had placed a special vest on him that blew up with air and then shook him slightly to break up the pneumonia in his lungs. Since he had been in such terrific shape, he was able to get out some good coughs.

We were all excited about his progress. His eyes opened now, and we talked to him while we were in his room. Kayla and I happened to both be there when Dr. Samaar walked in to check on Isaiah. We watched as Dr. Samaar grabbed one of the many stuffed animals that were gifts from friends and had come in handy to prop up Isaiah's legs and arms. Dr. Samaar made a quick motion towards Isaiah's face, watching to see if there was a blinking reaction. There was none.

I remember looking at Kayla across the bed from me and realizing that although his eyes were open, we had been talking to someone who was not really awake. Tears welled up in Kayla's eyes as she realized the same thing. Dr. Samaar looked at me and spoke kindly as he tried to let us know that this was going to be a long recovery. Not weeks, he said, but months of recovery.

I resisted the urge to yell, "No, you're wrong! He's going to pop out of this. Just wait and see. My God can do anything!" But I held it in. I knew all Jesus had to do was speak the word, and Isaiah would leap from that bed and be completely fine. But this was not His plan. At times I was frustrated about that fact, but then He would remind me that it was not what He had designed for Isaiah.

When I see Isaiah today, with his noticeable gait and slow right hand, I see them as reminders of what he has endured and how Jesus has used him to reach other people that otherwise he would have never met and influenced. They are reminders of God's grace in his life. The

Apostle Paul wrote about having a thorn in the flesh. He asked God three times to remove it, but when it was not healed, he said God's grace was sufficient. That is also what Isaiah believes.

Posted August 7, 2008, by Randy

I'm back! It seems like the only time I write is when it is quiet, which is late at night. Stacey and I didn't get here until around 9:00 p.m., and after hauling a few loads of "stuff" in from the car, we visited Isaiah, and that is where I will stay tonight.

Seeing Isaiah tonight was exciting, but seeing him fight to breathe or cough or open his eyes and look at me as if to say, "What is happening?" was tough. Before, he seemed comfortable when he was in a deeper coma. Don't take me wrong. These deep breaths, coughs, and movements are all great signs. The harder the cough the better. Tonight he is doing all that he should and more. Everyone who plays on the football team knows he always give it his best.

Stacey got an award at basketball camp as the most improved player. Great job, Stacey! In spite of everything that has happened in the last ten days, you still worked hard and gave it your all! Way to go!

As Isaiah continues to heal, we have come to understand that we have a long road ahead of us, so I am trying to take steps to move our adjusted family life in that direction. It has been a learning experience for me! For example, I didn't know that I wasn't supposed to fill that little hole in the washing machine to the brim with softener when using concentrated softener. I thought the stuff was disappearing fast, but the towels were really soft!

Then we made a mistake with some lady undergarments. Notice I said we. So I had to go shopping. If you go to Wal-Mart at 1:00 a.m., it is pretty quiet, but searching for the right garments was kind of nerve wracking. I didn't know there were so many styles and sizes!

Okay, I will stop. I'm not sure why I'm even telling you this, but it is all part of the adjustments. This is not an update but a sharing of life. I think I want people to understand, and that includes me, what families have to go through in a situation like this.

Once Isaiah was past the initial critical stage, the doctors could concentrate on his right cheek surgery and prepare him for rehab. During this time, they discharged him from the PICU, and that was a hard day. We had come to love these doctors, nurses, and staff. We'd been living there for the past three weeks, but now it was time to move to the regular pediatric floor and one step closer to rehab.

Isaiah went through the surgery on his right cheek with flying colors. Four titanium plates were used to reconstruct his sinus cavity and area around his right eye. Since his cheek bone had been crushed they needed to use the titanium plates to rebuild his cheek and also around his eye. To do this they inserted a needle through the inside of his upper lip and just outside his right eye. They squeezed his skin together to pull it out of the way to get to his bone underneath. When he returned to his room, he looked as if he'd been in a boxing match. Although his eyes were open now, he was still unaware of what was going on. He would smile but not respond to any of us.

The physical therapists came in daily and helped him sit on the side of his bed. He was unable to hold up his own head, but they worked his legs and arms, bending them this way and that. I thought it had to feel good for him to be upright after lying in the bed for so long. They also strapped him to a table that elevated him into an upright position and allowed him to be up for about ten minutes at a time. Then it was back to his bed.

We noticed he was moving his left arm and left leg quite a bit, but there was not much movement on his right side, which worried us. The doctors were also keeping track of his lack of movement on his right side. They placed a GT tube (a tube surgically placed through his abdomen directly into his stomach, with a balloon on the inside to help hold it in place) into his stomach, and this is how he would be fed until he could eat on his own since he was unable to swallow yet.

We had purchased an inexpensive CD player in order to play Isaiah's favorite music. While he rested, we turned on the Kutless *Strong Tower* CD. He used to listen to this in his car all the time, and his favorite song was their cover song, "Strong Tower."

Some dear friends had bracelets made for Isaiah. They wanted everyone back home to remember to pray for him when he left for rehabilitation. Tony found the verse that said it all. It was the verse from Proverbs 18:10: *"The name of the Lord is a strong tower. The righteous run to it and are safe."* Using the school colors, they had Isaiah's name and this scripture reference inscribed on the black-and-gold bracelets, and it was a reminder for many to continue to pray for a full recovery.

Once his cheek surgery was done and the GT tube inserted into his stomach, we were looking at possible rehabilitations centers where he would go for inpatient rehab. It was difficult to know which center would be best and even which center would accept him at the stage he was in. On the Glasgow Coma Scale Isaiah was at a "one" in verbal response. He would look around but not focus directly on anyone, and he had no control over his limbs; they only moved sporadically.

On the Rancho Cognitive Scale, a scale which measures levels of cognitive or mental functioning, Isaiah was at a level three. Many rehabs won't take patients at this stage because they require more care and aren't good candidates yet for performing in their physical, occupational, and speech therapies.

So here we were, wondering where Isaiah should go and who would agree to take him. There was also the issue of who had an open space. We felt so completely out of our comfort zone, with no idea what to look for in a rehab or which center had the best program for our son.

And then God placed me in the right place at the right time. I "happened" to overhear a couple talking in the family lounge about their 13-year-old daughter who had gone to Chicago for rehab. I asked them some questions about the place, and from their responses, it seemed like an excellent institute. We now felt we basically had two choices: the center in Iowa or the one in Chicago.

Dr. Samaar Kamath contacted them both for us and knew all the right questions to ask them. As a result, he informed us that if there was an opening and if it worked for us to go there, Chicago would be the best possible place for rehab. After much prayer, we talked to the insurance company. An empty spot and their willingness to pay for it would have to take place. Not only that, but Isaiah would have to be past the lower stages on the Glasgow Coma Scale. When he was brought in, he was at a one, which meant there had been no responsiveness in either opening his eyes, motor responses, or verbal response. There was much to take before the Lord. Normally, insurance only covers rehabs that are in-state. However, Isaiah's circumstances were a little different. Since Isaiah was working when the accident happened, he would be under workman's compensation. Randy contacted the representative and she said she would get back in touch with him. We wanted to take Isaiah to Chicago as it is one of the premiere rehabs in the country but it did not look promising.

Randy put out the word, and many people prayed for guidance for us. It was just a few minutes later that the case manager came back and said the Rehabilitation Institute of Chicago had an opening, and Isaiah could go there within three days! The power of prayer together with God's providence was becoming more and more evident.

We were so excited that Isaiah was going to be able to get the best rehab in the country, but then there were all the good-byes and the separation from family. For the most part, I would stay with Isaiah in Chicago. Stacey had started high school and would be without me for an unknown amount of time, and Kayla had started her college classes as well. Tony's new police chief had worked it out so that he could do his academy training at a facility closer to home so he would be able to be at home with Randy and Stacey. It would just be a season for our family to be apart. God was still on His throne and still very much involved in our lives.

Chapter Six
Inpatient Rehab

*A*fter many tears and hugs good-bye to the rest of the family, Randy and I followed the ambulance carrying Isaiah on the five-hour drive to the Rehabilitation Institute of Chicago. It was exactly one month since Isaiah had been flown to Iowa City. Now, on August 27th, we were leaving this more familiar place to face the unknown ahead.

Every so often as we followed the ambulance, we could see Isaiah's left foot come up in the air. Apparently, his legs had been unstrapped for awhile to give him a more comfortable ride. Up to this point, he had only been moving his left arm and leg and only rarely and slowly moving his right arm.

We are from a small farming community in Iowa. Silos are the tallest structures where we live, so entering the heart of Chicago with its tall skyscrapers made us a bit uncomfortable. There are so many people living in the Windy City, and traffic noise is constant. We gazed at this urban landscape and realized this would be my home for an undetermined amount of time.

It was early afternoon when we arrived in downtown Chicago. Nervously, we entered the 18-story Rehabilitation Institute of Chicago. From its windows we could see Lake Michigan and Navy Pier. If this had been a fun family weekend, it would have been more of a beautiful sight. But for me, this only meant separation from Randy, Stacey, Kayla, and Tony. Five hours away seemed more like one hundred hours away to me.

The staff got us settled into Isaiah's room, and Dr. Charles Sisung entered. He introduced himself and began to examine Isaiah. Up to this point, Isaiah had not spoken a word or even made a sound. He would look at us without really seeing us and perform simple commands like raising his left arm if asked, but nothing more complicated than that.

It was difficult to see just how thin Isaiah had become. Only a month earlier he was a strapping 215-pound football player, strong and muscular. Now he was a very thin 156 pounds with dark circles around his sunken eyes. He looked more like a marathon runner than a football player.

After only a few brief looks, Dr. Sisung proceeded to inform us that within six to eight weeks they would have Isaiah able to eat on his own and possibly walking and talking. Randy and I glanced at each other, doubtful and yet encouraged to hear him say this could all be a real possibility.

Randy began to explore places for me to stay over the next weeks or months. Although I could sleep on the couch in Isaiah's room, we would need a bit more space when the rest of the family came to visit. Randy called the Ronald McDonald House to see if they had any openings and was told the waiting list was usually two weeks or more. What were we going to do? Randy decided to take the car and drive around to see what hotels were close to the rehab institute with available rooms.

Now if we were back in Iowa, this would not be that difficult, but we were not in Iowa, where a person can see for miles. He headed towards Michigan Avenue. As he drove, he searched for hotel signs only to realize there would be no "seeing" them, at least not without looking up!

Gazing heavenward, he suddenly became aware that the traffic light in front of him had turned red, and he quickly pushed on the brakes. He was on top of the pedestrian walkway and was getting some angry looks from those having to walk around the car. Randy decided to pull out the map to make it look like he was lost, which he was. He thought they might have a bit more compassion for him if they thought he was an out-of-towner.

He did eventually find us a place to stay for that evening just a few blocks away from rehab. It was one of the toughest nights I would have in the Windy City. Leaving Isaiah there with total strangers, and yet needing to spend time with my husband before he returned home left me torn and frightened.

As soon as we settled into our room, I broke down. How was this going to work? In a few days, I would be alone in a strange city, not knowing anyone and completely away from anything normal to me. Had we made a wrong decision? We questioned our decision for only a moment and then Randy hugged me and reminded me that in the grand scheme of things, this was only for a short time, and for Isaiah's recovery and future, this was the best place for him. As I looked out the fifth floor window at all the city lights and listened to the buzzing traffic below, I thought of the thousands of people out there, and yet I felt so alone. I would have to get through this.

We got to the institute early the next morning because they wasted no time getting Isaiah into his therapy sessions. At 7:30 a.m. he went down for his first physical therapy workout. For an hour they worked to help him stand in front of his wheelchair. Then they gave him time to rest during the session since he tired easily. After each break, I brought him back to his room, and he would sleep for an hour.

For his occupational therapy, they brought in a magazine and toothbrush on a platter and asked Isaiah which he would use to brush his teeth. He was not focused at all, looking around the room and bobbing his head. They asked him the same question several more times, and he finally grabbed the toothbrush. I could not tell if it was because he actually knew what it was, or if the toothbrush just happened to be closest to his left hand.

After lunch, Isaiah went for an hour of speech therapy. They ran some swallowing tests on him to evaluate whether or not he could start on pureed foods but found he was still having some difficulty swallowing, so he remained on the chocolate-milk-looking substance coming through his G-Tube.

I think the hardest part of Isaiah not being able to swallow was his constant drooling. The weather that September was beautiful, and in the afternoons we tried to get him outside in his wheelchair for awhile. People passing by on the sidewalks seemed busy and so normal—and then there was us. As people walked by, I noticed many either looked away or acted like they hadn't seen us, and if Isaiah had a long string of saliva hanging from his mouth, people would stare. At that point I made a vow that I would never again look at people in wheelchairs the same way. They are people with feelings just like anyone else, and they don't deserve to be ignored or stared at. These were all part of the lessons God was teaching my family and me, and I would never forget them.

While I attended the therapies with Isaiah, Randy checked out the rest of the rehab facility. He also talked with other families about where they had found lodging. He had been in contact with the Ronald McDonald House but was not having any luck. Frustrated, he wrote on the care pages about our need for a room in Chicago, some place where it wouldn't cost an arm and a leg. By 3:00 p.m., the Ronald McDonald House contacted Randy and informed him they had a room available for us that could sleep four to five people. God had provided in a mighty way! It was a relief for Randy to know that I would have a good bed to rest in. He also purchased bus tickets for me from the Ronald McDonald House to rehab and back. It was about three miles away, and I would only have to walk five blocks all together.

By our third day in Chicago, Isaiah was already standing between the parallel bars during PT time. I believe he really liked being upright because we had to watch him closely. We would try to transfer him from his wheelchair to the bed, and he would randomly stand up. He was wobbly, but he was determined to stand, so between Tony and Randy, they helped give him the support to stand for a few minutes.

Randy, Tony, Kayla, and Stacey were all with me the first weekend. It was the first time that just the five of us had been together with Isaiah, and it felt so good to have them there. We walked down to Navy Pier and along the walkway that overlooks the beach area. It was a beautiful weekend.

I know it was difficult for the kids to see their brother in a wheelchair and drooling all the time. Kayla was constantly busy wiping his mouth for him, and Tony and Stacey took turns pushing him.

We spent the night together in the one room of the Ronald McDonald House and had a really good heart-to-heart talk with each of them about how they were dealing with the whole situation. It was hard on all of them. They just wanted their brother back. Many tears were shed and hugs given out, but it was part of the healing process for all of us. At this point I don't believe I had totally allowed my grief to float to the surface. I was still in a survival mode and doing whatever I needed to do.

I would have liked the weekend to last longer, but they all had to get back to work.

Posted September 1, 2008, by Ranae

"The Lord is near. Be anxious for nothing, but in everything by prayer and supplication with thanksgiving let your requests be made known to God. And the peace that surpasses all comprehension will guard your hearts and minds in Christ Jesus." Philippians 4: 5-7.

It is never too late to call out to God and ask Him to reveal Himself to you. He gets a lot better reception that any wireless company I know! In the middle of the night, He is there; in the deepest deep, He is there; in the highest high, He is there. There will never be a time when He is NOT available. NEVER!

We are not the only ones with struggles in this life. Being in places like the University of Iowa Hospitals and the rehab institute here in Chicago, we hear heart-wrenching stories that don't always turn out the way people wanted, or their problems are multiplied in many different directions. All I can say is that it's never too late to call out to Him and allow Him space in our lives. He wants to walk these tough paths with us if we only allow Him to. He won't barge His way in. He will only come if He's invited. He's just waiting.

We did get Isaiah back outside today, and he loves it! He looks around at everything and is doing a lot better at swallowing, so we don't have to keep wiping his mouth for him. In fact, when the girls were trying to help him out in that area, he grabbed hold of the wash cloth, put it in his mouth, and bit down on it. As if to say, "I'll just keep it there!"

Tony even got an undeserved slug today. He and Randy were helping Isaiah sit on the side of the bed. Randy had his arm around Isaiah, and it was touching his front nipple area. Isaiah looked at Tony and slugged him with a smile on his face. Tony said, "What was that for?" When we figured it out, we told Isaiah to go ahead and give Tony a pinch, and he did!

After Randy and the kids left, an overwhelming feeling started to creep in on me. I wondered about Isaiah's future. Would he ever speak? What would he be able to do? Every evening when I returned to the Ronald McDonald House, I read my Bible. It never failed to calm my fears and encourage me. On one particular night, when I was feeling worried and far from my family and missing them, this verse was the one I read:

"Do not worry about tomorrow, for tomorrow will worry about itself." Matthew 6:34.

I knew God was comforting me and telling me I didn't need to worry because He had Isaiah and had plans for him. Now, it's not always easy for a mom not to worry, but I decided to try my best and leave the rest up to God. I trusted Him to let me in on things whenever He was good and ready. Holding onto this assurance, I would drift off to sleep and not wake up until I heard the alarm.

I'm shaking my head as I write down these things because it's so clear in hindsight that things kept happening with His help and according to His plan. For example, I hadn't been at the rehab for more than a week when a young woman walked into Isaiah's room over lunch. She asked if I was Ranae and told me that I might know her parents. Come to find out, her mom and dad had attended our small church back in Lakota before we moved to Shell Rock. I knew them well but hadn't realized their daughter worked in Chicago. Not only did she work in Chicago, she worked right across the street! I had a connection to home right under my nose! God is SO GOOD!

Deb came several times a week over her lunch break to visit with me and with Isaiah when he wasn't asleep. It was such a great feeling to have a friend and someone who knew the downtown area. She gave me ideas about where I should take Isaiah on our daily outdoor excursions.

As Isaiah improved, Deb walked with me as I pushed Isaiah in his wheelchair to Michigan Avenue to the Hershey Store. Another day we walked down to the Chicago River and crossed the bridge to Millennium Park. It was a long walk pushing Isaiah in the wheelchair, but it was fun to see the different sites in Chicago. I was so grateful for Deb's friendship and the conversations we had. Isaiah wasn't talking yet, so it was refreshing to have another adult to talk to.

Posted September 4, 2008 by Ranae

Today was not a huddle for the football team but for the team of doctors who are in charge of Isaiah's case. They call it huddle time to discuss his initial evaluation and what they see as a potential end date. All of the therapists said they couldn't believe the progress he's made just over the weekend, and they hadn't even done an official session with him yet!

They are talking six weeks, give or take, depending on how well Isaiah is doing and progressing. I think he set out today to try to meet some of those goals as he did 4 hours of therapy this morning starting at 9:00. He impressed Catie in PT with how helpful he could be getting into his own chair and then actually sitting on the side of the table mat, feet on the floor, hands at his sides to steady himself, all by himself, without anyone touching him!

His speech therapy went better today as well since he did better at swallowing quicker than yesterday. It takes him about 3–5 seconds to swallow. However, the longer she tries to get him to do it, his attention span becomes shorter, and he's distracted by all the other things going on around the room. She said this is normal with brain trauma patients.

We also played 3-way catch, and Isaiah did well catching the ball. He just hasn't gotten down the release part yet. I keep thinking that's because he doesn't want to fumble the ball!

It was interesting this afternoon. Isaiah got to stand in a special piece of equipment that he sits in. Then they strap his feet and waist down and proceed to crank him to a standing position with support at the knees and chest for balance. He stood there for a whole twelve minutes on both legs! While he stood there, he played three games of Connect 4 with the occupational therapist. He is getting this game down!

It was a little harder to leave him there tonight because he is getting more restless as he becomes more aware of what's going on around him. I prayed with him before I left, and he grabbed my arm and started rubbing it. I think he knew I was headed out for the night. I think from now on I will wait to leave until he is sleeping.

Posted September 7, 2008 by Ranae

I was reading to Isaiah from my devotional today, and the verse they used is one I'm sure we've all heard many times, but today it struck a new cord in me. John 3:16: "For God so loved the world that He gave His one and only Son, that whoever believed in Him should not perish but have everlasting life." In the devotional reading, it talked about looking to see where God was in this difficult time and what He was trying to accomplish. It struck me again that God has plans for us, and He always proves Himself much bigger than I imagine. The people he has placed here at the rehab to give words of encouragement are directly from Him.

I believe even the taxi driver said she would pray for Isaiah and to expect great things to happen if God is in this! It's really weird and hard to put into words, but I am not afraid, for I know He is watching over me. As Pastor John would say, "He's got my back!"

I stand every day and watch Isaiah impress the therapists with his determination and desire to get better. Today, he didn't take long to pick out his first name, his last name, state, and birth date during SPT, as if to say, "Is that all you got?" He did fine with his swallowing, but it still needs to improve more because he still does about ten swallows and then gets distracted.

I think he really likes PT because when she comes in, he lights up and even gave her a knuckle bump today. He sat by himself for almost ten minutes on the mat and even played catch with me while doing it. He was able to keep his balance and sit up much straighter. Then she worked his leg muscles, and he did some moving with his right leg. It is very exciting to see him using the right arm and leg. He even picked up some rubber rings with his right hand today and placed them on the cone!

And if that was not enough for one day, God always goes beyond and brings MAIL! I just shook my head, and tears came, as they are now, at the kindness shown to Isaiah. I told him he had mail, and he began reaching for it and opened three envelopes on his own. He pulled out the cards and handed them to me to read. He sat and listened to them, and I couldn't hold back the tears. I've really tried to be strong in front of him, but this time the tears were of pure joy. He put his hand on my back and rubbed my arm. I think he knew I was overwhelmed with gratefulness.

After being at the Institute for close to three weeks it was amazing to see the almost-daily progress Isaiah was making, but he still had not spoken or even made any kind of sound. It was difficult not to have him ever respond to me. As he looked at me, I felt he wanted to say something but couldn't find his voice to be able to get it out. I thought how frustrating this must be for him to feel trapped inside his mind and being unable to communicate his feelings, his pain, or his fear of what had happened to him.

I reminded him every morning about the accident. I wasn't sure if he totally understood where he was or if he even realized that he had been in a bad car accident. The doctors kept encouraging me to retell the events until the time came when he understood what had happened.

Since Isaiah was 16, he was placed on the pediatric floor. We saw many young people with injuries, and their families struggling with their own personal trials. The stories of once-vibrant youth who now fought for breath or couldn't walk brought hurt for so many. This is where God had brought us, and I wanted to be used by Him to reach out to the other mothers who were staying there with their children.

It's strange how circumstances can bond complete strangers, but that is what happened. We, as parents of injured children, bonded as we shared the daily ups and downs with each other. It wasn't uncommon to share a hug in the laundry room where we took turns keeping up with our dirty clothes, or to give an encouraging smile as we watched another teen trying so hard to sit on the side of the table in physical therapy.

One thing I learned about Isaiah during this whole time was that he is a very determined young man. I don't believe he liked being in the wheelchair because as I was getting ready to head to one of his therapies, he decided to arch his back and slide out from under the seatbelt. After I tried to stop him and failed, all I could do was struggle to keep him from falling onto the floor. When I saw one of the staff pass by in the hallway, I called for help. He decided to add extra straps to Isaiah's legs so that wouldn't happen again.

For the first few weeks, Isaiah enjoyed physical therapy. They placed him between two parallel bars and, using a gait belt, helped him stand on his legs for short periods of time. Then he would sit back down in the chair. They also had him lie down on the padded, elevated table, and he would roll back and forth on a soft cylinder ball. In another exercise, he had to balance himself on all fours. It took a lot of concentration in the beginning, but little by little he continued to improve.

In order for PT to initially trick his brain into remembering to walk, they hooked Isaiah up with a harness that reminded me of a parachute which was strapped to a LiteGait Walker. Electric patches were placed on his right leg so they could send electric currents through his leg to expand and contract his muscles. As one PT slowly pushed the gait walker ahead, the other sent the electric shocks through Isaiah's muscles.

The look on his face was priceless! He still wasn't talking, but his expression was saying *"What are you doing to me?"* This process took a few times over a period of days before his right leg started firing on its own. He was then able to be strapped behind a smaller walker that allowed him to take steps at his own pace without the electric shocks.

Christie, Isaiah's occupational therapist, would come into the room and work to get him to use his right hand. One morning she entered before he had gotten dressed because her plan was to have him put on his own shirt and take it off. He gave me a look of shock! Although he was not talking yet, I understood "the look." His modesty had kicked in, and he really didn't want to take off his shirt in front of her. I assured him it was okay and that this was part of his therapy and after a bit more prodding, he did remove his shirt and put it back on for her. It was slow going, but he had accomplished it, mostly using his left hand.

Christie also played Connect Four with him. The only stipulation was he needed to use his right hand to put the pieces onto the board. It took a bit, but he carefully placed them in the slots and did a very good job with thinking through his strategy. I was encouraged to see him actually calculating a strategy because I wasn't sure how he was processing information. This was a terrific sign to me that he was able to plan and think ahead.

Speech therapy was probably the most difficult and the most frustrating for him. He might swallow eight to ten times on his own, but then he'd get distracted and not be able to swallow as well. As long as he was not swallowing, he was not allowed to eat pureed food. The only time he could eat "real" food was in the presence of Vicki, the speech therapist. She was not one to give up easily! She tried to give him a spicy, flaming-hot cheeto. Of course, Isaiah wanted food, so he picked it up and quickly stuffed it into his mouth. She waited for him to scream or make any kind of noise. But nothing.

On another occasion, she left and came back with an ice cube and dropped it down his back! Still no sound came from his mouth. He wasn't quite sure what to think of Vicki, but I think he also knew she was the "food lady" and wanted her to bring him some food to eat.

Posted September 10, 2008 by Ranae

When I got to the rehab today, Isaiah was still sleeping, and as he slept, I watched him and prayed. It's been so long since I've heard his voice, and with each day and week that passes, it gets harder not to hear him talk. I've been doing most of my Bible reading in the book of Isaiah. These verses jumped off the page at me this morning: "They will see the glory of the LORD, the splendor of our God. Strengthen the feeble hands, STEADY the knees that give way; say to those with fearful hearts, 'BE STRONG, do not fear; your God will come, he will come with vengeance; with divine retribution He will come to save you.' Then will the lame leap like a deer, and the MUTE TONGUE SHOUT FOR JOY!" Isaiah 35: 2b-6

Of course, these verses are dealing with the future of the people of Israel, but the references to the knees and tongue really struck me. I'm praying that

Isaiah will find his voice again in order to shout for joy what the LORD ALMIGHTY has done for him.

At the end of each day, after Isaiah was down for the night, I would either catch the shuttle bus or take a cab back to the Ronald McDonald House. It was so lonely, and my biggest connection to home was on the care pages. Although I couldn't wait to update everyone about Isaiah's progress and what was happening, I also absolutely adored all the messages sent back to us. Many people wrote about how inspirational our posts were, but, to me, my inspiration came from others. Their notes of encouragement or verses written out to help us cope with life were so beneficial to me.

When morning came, my daily routine was to wake up at 5:30 a.m., get dressed, head down to the community kitchen, and eat a bowl of oatmeal. I also used mornings to read my Bible. The funny thing was, only a year earlier I had done a study on the book of Isaiah. At the time I thought I was studying it to prepare something for the group of girls I was leading at church. Little did I realize that God would use that study to bring about some of my greatest comforts and encouragement.

I am in awe to this day of how great the power of His word is. It is living and active and able to cut into the core of our being. It penetrates to the deepest parts of our souls and is so integral to who we are. There is no other substitute that can fill our void like His Word. Although this should have been one of the lowest points in my life, I actually had never felt closer to His presence, and I can't wait for the day He returns for me!

Posted September 11, 2008 by Ranae

It was a beautiful day here, and I decided to get Isaiah out as soon as he was done with therapy. He had another good day in his progress. His SPT decided to try to jump start his talking by giving him a bit of really hot cheetos. You should have seen the look on his face! She really wanted him to make some kind of noise, but all he could do was grab the nearest washcloth and stick it into his mouth! After that, he didn't open his mouth for her again. Wonder why?! Maybe he'll forget by tomorrow.

His PT went well as he got up on his hands and knees and did some work on his right leg and arm. I think he must have gotten a workout because once she was done, he lay down, and we had a hard time getting him back up. She also had him working on his abs, and he did well with that. If he can get his ab muscles built up, it will help him in his sitting and standing. He sat for almost two minutes by himself for the OT this morning, so that is getting better every day.

Now that he is getting more mobile, I have to keep a watch on him because he pushes his own chair with his left hand and leg, and he's getting good at not running into anything. I told him we were going to go outside, so I went to get his coat and my cell phone, and money for ice cream. When I looked out into the hallway, he was gone! He was down around two corners, trying to find the door that leads to outside! We went out for about two hours and tried to get some ice cream, but McDonald's was out.

I continued reading in Isaiah chapter 36 this morning and was struck by the comments King Sennecherib sent out to King Hezekiah. He taunted him and told the people that they shouldn't listen to him because his God couldn't save them from the king of Assyria. Well, you'll have to read it to find out what King Sennecherib found out (The rest of the story!). It encouraged me as it always did in the mornings. Sometimes it's hard not to wonder if there will be any improvements for the day, and doubt creeps in. Satan would like us to think our God can't save us or help us in our time of need, and he taunts us with similar words. We can either allow them to defeat us, or we can run to God and ask Him for help. He is always faithful.

Posted September 14, 2008 by Randy

"The Lord is near. Be anxious for nothing, but in everything, by prayer and supplication with thanksgiving, let your requests be made known to God. And the peace of God, which surpasses all comprehension, will guard your hearts and minds in Christ Jesus." Philippians 4:5-7.

"Be anxious for nothing…" But God, I want him home and back with us now, if you know what I mean.

"But in everything, by prayer and supplication with thanksgiving, present your requests to God." As we hit our knees with requests and thanksgiving, Isaiah is trying to stand and walk, giving it his all.

Stacey, Cody, Ranae, and I have been having a great weekend with Isaiah. Still, it always hits me a bit when I first see Isaiah and his limitations, so different from the son I once walked alongside while pheasant hunting. I'd tell Tony to back off and give his younger brother a chance to shoot first before the two of us "cleaned up." It didn't take long, though, before Isaiah was on his own!

I once might have casually said to Isaiah, "Let's jump on our motorcycles and take a ride for an hour." Now I hear myself more anxiously say, "Isaiah, you can do it! You can move your foot! lift your hand! swallow! take a step! " And then God's peace kicks in again.

As I was reviewing pictures of Isaiah on the camera, I was reminded of God's hand in our lives. God has spared Isaiah's life, and he has continued to improve each day. I remember parents supporting their children in Iowa City when their children were not having a good day. The road for them had been 3, 5, even 7 long years. I asked myself, 'Why not Isaiah? Why not our family? Who said we would not have trials in this life?'

As I sit here typing this, a family is meeting behind me. They are talking about Isaiah and how his inspiration with his recovery has challenged their son to move forward. Their son watches Isaiah in the gym and now tries to do the things Isaiah can do, and they challenge their son to follow his example. WOW! Lord, may my son always be such a positive inspiration to others that they will want to follow his example.

Then this morning as Isaiah was getting back into bed for a rest, he pulled both his legs up to his chest as he rolled over to position himself. It seems so small, but it's a sign of more movement with his right leg. He stands up with no problem and is smart enough that he has learned to adjust his balance. So part of the therapy is to force him to use his right side more and continue to stimulate his brain to use those muscles.

As for eating, I think he is ready and willing. We will have to pursue that area with the doctors. He has been eating with his SPT therapist. Continue to pray for words as he seems so close. He has made a few moans, but no words yet.

Posted September 16, 2008 by Ranae

El bano! I don't know how many of you know what those words mean, but we practiced today, allowing Isaiah to get up and down in the bathroom. He was grinning the whole time! He is doing much better with the tasks of putting on his clothes and brushing his teeth and washing his face. He got to go up to the 15th floor to work with the technology department , and they hooked him up with sheets that have words on them to help him communicate what he is feeling until he starts talking. He did well in pointing to the words when they asked him questions. The one that brought comfort to me was when they asked him how he was feeling today. He pointed to "happy"! Proverbs 17:22a says, "A cheerful heart is like medicine." I guess Isaiah has a cheerful heart!

One of the fellows who is working with Isaiah stopped me in the hall today to say they were all amazed at the progress he was making and the determination he had. He said it was rubbing off on the other young men with similar injuries. He told me he could not believe how Isaiah seemed to be handling all the challenges he had been dealt. It was so encouraging to talk with him because he has obviously seen a lot while working here. All I can say is, 'Praise the Almighty God who was and who is and who is to come.' He is the One who has done these things, and we will give Him the glory for all of it!

My blog updates were usually hopefully optimistic, but I have to admit there would be days when I would be so down. This whole process was so long, and all the time away from Randy and Stacey sometimes got to me. Stacey was right in the middle of volleyball season. And football was well underway. This was probably working on my mind as well. I kept wondering if Isaiah realized he was missing his junior year of football or if he would ever be able to do anything like that again.

Whenever these feelings swelled inside me, I can remember hearing God's voice in my head saying, *"My grace is sufficient for you."* So I would commit to trusting Him again to help me get through another day.

We'd been on the pediatric floor now for several weeks, and Isaiah was getting so anxious to eat some real food. I never thought he would resort to stealing, but the day came! We were sitting around the dining room table doing a game in a group OT session when one young man and his mom came up to join the group.

Jack, who had injuries to his brain similar to Isaiah's, had just come back from Subway. His mother was also trying to get him to eat and thought a sandwich would help. Isaiah spotted it, and without even taking the brakes off his wheelchair, pushed with all his might to get around the table. I kept asking him where he was going, and all at once I realized his intentions!

He grabbed the sandwich and started to reach for his mouth when we all heard in a loud, clear voice, "No!" Jack had decided he wanted to eat the sandwich, and Isaiah had just taken it from him. Thankfully, Isaiah decided to give the sandwich back, and a wonderful friendship began between Jack and Isaiah and Jack's mom, Jane, and me.

Posted September 18, 2008 by Ranae

Sorry this is a little late in coming, but the one computer at the house was busy until way past my bed time! We had a good laugh yesterday during SPT. Vicki asked Isaiah what mood he was in, and he pointed to the happy face on the cards they had made for him. She asked to see his happy face. He smiled broadly, and I got it on camera. Then she asked to see his mad and sad faces. He complied with both requests, and we laughed at his expressions because he enjoyed the attention he was getting.

He ate the whole plate of scrambled eggs and sausage she brought for him, and she's hoping to get him some meals by the end of this week or first part of next week.

He walked through the halls yesterday with the help of a tall walker that he could rest his arms on and with grips to hold onto with his hands. He only needed a little cuing with his right leg, but otherwise he did it on his own!

When he sat to rest, the therapist had him kick his right leg and also do some marching moves with his right leg as he sat in his chair. It was so exciting to see him using his right leg.

This morning we had our first experience with using the restroom facilities, and let me just say…we had a touchdown! He's going to kill me some day for putting it out there, but I think I can handle it! It's amazing how God provides the strength we need when we need it and also provides the little things we don't even ask for.

When I got back to the Ronald McDonald House, they had corn on the cob! I have been craving it since the season was just starting when the accident happened, and I hadn't had any. As I was downing my third ear, it hit me. God had known I was craving something as insignificant as this, and here he provided it. Is He wonderful or what?

P.S. I'm really hoping the meal they're promising Isaiah comes quickly because last night they had dogs working with the patients, and the patients got to hand out doggie treats when the dogs performed correctly. Isaiah misses eating so badly that even dog treats look good! No, he didn't eat one, but it was close. It's just a good thing I was looking and caught him in time!

Family Portrait 1997, L to R, Ranae, Stacey,
Randy, Isaiah, Tony, and Kayla

Isaiah's freshmen football, #40

Isaiah and friend, Cody, at freshmen science fair, 2007

2008 Prom

The vehicle Isaiah was riding in the back of

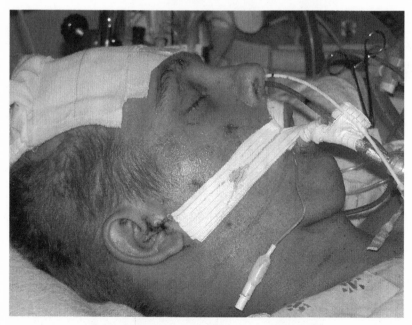

Isaiah in University of Iowa Children's
Hospital, the first week in PICU

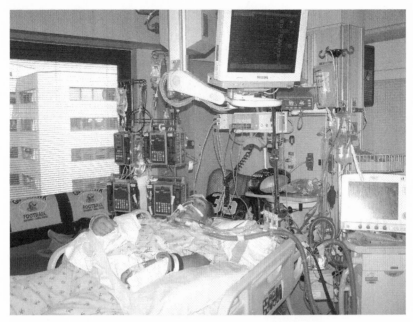

Isaiah in University of Iowa Children's
Hospital, the first week in PICU

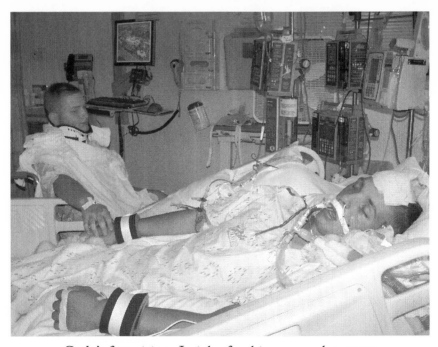

Cody's first visit to Isaiah after his own neck surgery

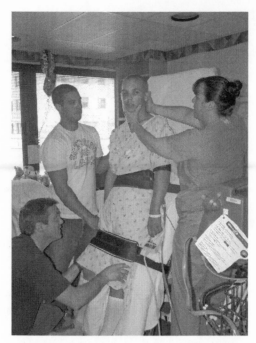

First time being upright in three weeks

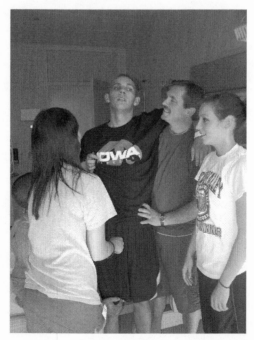

First weekend with just family in Chicago Rehab

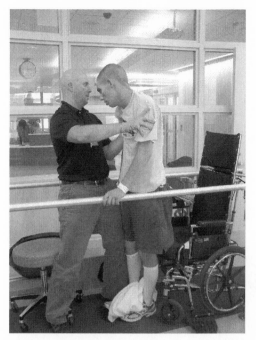

Physical Therapy Session, trying to stand

Occupational Therapy- trying to use right hand

Speech Therapy- learning to swallow and talk

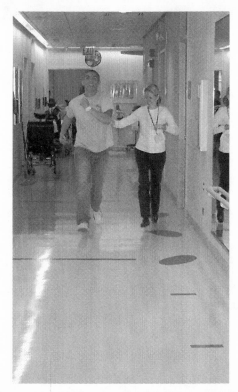

November 2008- the week before returning
home, jogging down the halls!

2009 Homecoming King

April, 2010- Witnessing Gov. Culver sign
the backseat belt bill into law

May, 2010- Isaiah's high school graduation speech

Mrs. Kathy Whitney, Randy, Isaiah, Ranae, and Dave Arns.
Isaiah receives the Exchange Club District ACE Award in
Omaha, NE. (A-accepting the C-challenge of E-excellence)

Our family, R- Tony (holding new daughter, Tinley Faith) with wife, Bailey, holding Kinnick on her lap, in front. Behind- Kayla beside her husband David, and Stacey. Front-R- Ranae, Randy, and Isaiah.

Chapter Seven
Isaiah Speaks

God, and God Alone!
Posted September 19, 2008 at 7:59 p.m. by Ranae

"God, and God alone, created all these things we call our own. God, and God alone, is fit to take the universe's throne! It's God's and God's alone!" This little snippet from a song came to mind to me today as I sat in speech therapy and heard Isaiah make his first sound in almost eight weeks! Not ten minutes before his therapy, he woke up from a nap, and I told him I wanted to pray for God to loose his tongue and vocal cords and whatever He needed to do to get him to talk.

As I heard him make the e-e-e-e-e-e sound following the speech therapist's command, all I could do was cry and thank our AWESOME GOD! I feel so insignificant, and yet the God who sits on the throne of the universe answered the prayer of one, small creature like me. I'm blown away!

He looked at the therapist, and his time was almost done. She asked him to say, "Bye, Vicki," and he did!

He's not talking my leg off, but he is definitely trying to make his words come out. He is becoming more aware of what's going on. Every day I still tell him about the accident and that he has been in the hospital and is now in Chicago. Today, when I told him he had been in the hospital, he looked a little worried. The therapist also noticed he is becoming more aware of things.

He let us know he needed to use the "facility" three times today. He is becoming more stable when standing, which helps when he needs to use the bathroom. He also gained 8 pounds.

His first pureed meal came tonight, and he ate almost the whole thing. It was chicken, mashed potatoes and gravy, broccoli, pudding, and applesauce.

It is truly a testimony to the power of fervent prayers going up to our Heavenly Father on Isaiah's behalf. God bless each and every one of you.

*F*or me, this was a breakthrough. To hear Isaiah speak was the most blessed sound I had heard. After he'd made the "e" sound, she asked him to say "Mom." He did. She wanted me to ask him a question, but I was unable to say anything through all the tears.

Posted September 21, 2008 at 4:56 p.m. by Ranae

The devotional I'm reading said we must meditate on God's Word and not wait until tragedy strikes. This hit me because last summer I felt God wanted me to study the book of Isaiah. I thought, "Oh, He must have something in there for me to use on Wednesday nights for my small group."

So I studied Isaiah. Little did I know that this very book would be the one that has brought me the most comfort during this trial in our own lives. He knew all along this was going to happen and what words would bring the most comfort at just the right time.

Psalms 119:50: "This is my comfort in my affliction, that Your word has revived me."

Isaiah 26:3: "You will keep him in perfect peace whose mind is fixed on You…"

The more we study His Word, the more our perspective on things changes into viewing them the way He views them, and He thinks a lot more clearly than we do! It gives me a better way of approaching issues that come, and they have been coming, but I'm trusting in His Word.

This weekend has been wonderful with Tony, Kayla, and David. Isaiah was excited to see them, and today he was talking away to Tony. Not all of his words were easy to understand, but he remembered that Tony was working as a police officer, and he asked where Stacey was.

He got to walk with the walker, and when he first started out, he acted like he was going to take off running! The PT therapist told him to slow down just a bit so she could keep up with him. She did some work with him going up and down steps as well with the help of Tony by his side. A little extra muscle!

His right hand is still really weak. He is more aware of where he is and what happened. I believe he knows we're in Chicago. Tony asked if he wanted to go home and he replied, "Yes!"

The fervent prayer of a righteous man avails much, so thank you for praying.

As Isaiah continued to heal and progress, I did my daily reading in the book of Isaiah in the mornings before I left to catch the shuttle bus. Isaiah 63:7 encouraged me one morning as I read, "I will tell of the kindnesses of the LORD, the deeds for which He is to be praised, according to all the LORD has done for us--yes, many good things he has done."

I wanted to exclaim from the roof tops how much Jesus had done and continued to do. I realized how complex our bodies are and how fragile and yet He has the power to heal--maybe not always as we expect, but still He heals, from our bodies to our souls. There is nothing that is impossible with God!

A few days after I had read this verse, Isaiah was sitting in his wheelchair, working in PT. There were glass windows separating the PT gym from the open reception area. Isaiah kept glancing out the window at what was going on out in the open space. There was a 14-year-old girl who was a patient because she had inhaled fumes from an aerosol can. The therapist lifted her onto an elevated table and allowed her some time to be upright for a while, but the expression on her face was one of pain.

Isaiah was concerned she might really be in pain. He looked from me to her and back again and was not paying attention to what the therapist wanted him to do. I asked him if he was worried about the young girl, and he nodded his head yes, so I told him we would pray for her when we got back to the room. I didn't want to be embarrassed by praying in front of the therapist, so I tried to pass it off. I know! It wasn't seizing the moment that God was giving me to be a witness to this young therapist and besides, Isaiah was not about to wait. So right there we prayed for healing and comfort for this young patient. It felt so wonderful to obey what God was tugging on Isaiah's heart to do. I had almost missed that opportunity to be a light. Although the PT therapist never said anything, I know she had to have been impacted. The rest was up to God.

Isaiah continued to speak a few words, but it was still difficult to understand him, and he was only able to say two or three words at a time. I was sure he knew who we were, but he had a hard time coming up with our names. If we gave him the beginning sounds, he came close to saying the right names, and then after a couple of tries, he would get them right.

Posted September 24, 2008 by Ranae

"I wanna get out!" That was Isaiah's comment when we came back to his room after meeting some people that come every Wednesday night for dog therapy. I thought he would be exhausted after such a busy day, but he turned his wheelchair around and headed back for the central desk. He tried to figure out how to get those magic doors to open that led to the outside!

He tried touching them, and when several other attempts didn't work, he tried brute strength to open them. That didn't work either! The gals at the desk just had to laugh because they know Isaiah likes to go outside.

We had our huddle meeting this morning with all the therapists and doctors. Isaiah was with me this time, and they said they were just amazed at how far he's come. Of course, they are equally impressed with his enthusiasm.

Today they had him go up and down a flight of stairs in the fire escape three times. He did really well with very little need for assistance. The PT therapist just had to keep reminding him that he had to go slower. He took Isaiah into the hallway and walked with him in the walker for one loop, and then he told Isaiah he was going to have him walk without anything except a hand on his arms. Isaiah did a lap with the therapist only hanging onto his arms. He has improved so much with his balance and walking, and he likes being upright and walking. The only problem now is that I really have to watch him when he needs help getting into and out of his chair because he pops up so quickly that I'm not always ready for him to stand up! I have to keep on my toes.

He is doing well with his self-care too. His transfers are so much easier because he does most of the work now. I'm just there to steady him a bit.

He worked on saying the months of the year and got a little confused on some of them, but with very little prompting he was able to say them. He still mumbles things, and the SPT therapist said she will be working with him to help him enunciate his words and find the right words he is looking for. He gets frustrated if he's trying to say something and I don't totally understand him.

By the end of September, the speech therapist was working hard to get Isaiah's words out more clearly, so she asked if we had any music CD's with us with some of Isaiah's favorite music. I told her we had been listening to the Kutless CD in his room and quickly got it for her. She said that the past memory of songs or poems can trigger words and help patients speak more clearly. Once she placed the CD into the player and began the song "Strong Tower," Isaiah immediately began to sing word-for-word along with the lyrics in a strong, clear voice. He closed his eyes and lifted his hands toward heaven. He was worshipping his Maker right there in SPT. As you might expect, I couldn't hold back the tears. I looked at the therapist as she smiled and nodded her head. She commented that she really liked the song and wondered where she might be able to purchase the CD.

It was amazing to me how Isaiah's past memory was so clear as he sang the song in very clear words. He was pronouncing them well enough for anyone to understand. She next had him sing along with some nursery rhymes and other little ditties, all of which he was able to sing clearly as well.

Even through his trials, Isaiah was able to worship Jesus. It reminded me that no matter how much or little we can talk, there is nothing that can stop us from worshipping God.

Posted September 27, 2008 at 8:18 p.m. by Randy

There is a daily devotional book by Charles Stanley called <u>God Is in Control</u>. As I sat by Isaiah's side this evening, I opened it to a page called "Perfect Faith." In Hebrews it says faith is being sure of what we hope for and certain of what we do not see. In this book he states that God isn't satisfied with a little faith, or even great faith. He wants perfect faith.

God wants us to live in absolute confidence--unwavering, unswerving, and confidence--that if he says He's going to do something, we know He's going to do it! It doesn't make any difference whether or not the world agrees. Wow! Perfect faith! Trusting in Him to carry us on this journey, to lean on Him, turn all our worries over to Him, and abide in Him.

We had an awesome day today with 19 visitors! We allowed Isaiah to skip SPT so he could walk down to Navy Pier with his friends. He was so excited to see them and mess around with some of his buddies. We even ventured down to Lake Michigan, and as others waded in the water, Isaiah joined them by standing in one spot with some help. Nothing but smiles!

He looked at mom and me and asked if we dared him to take him out further! At times, Isaiah's speech is hard to understand, yet at other times it is very clear. I was humbled as I was putting his socks and shoes back on. He leaned over to me and said, "Dad, I will swim again!" If only everyone had that determination.

We know God is doing a great work through Isaiah, and all He asks us to do is have perfect faith. God's Got It! Pray for Isaiah's strength on his right side and the words to flow. All the things that Isaiah needs to improve on can only come from Him. No medication, no surgery, nothings we can do can help him heal. Healing will come through Jesus.
Thank you.
Randy, filling in for Ranae this week

That was the week I went home to spend some time with our three children. As hard as it was to leave Isaiah and Randy in Chicago, I was excited to see the rest of the family. It was a long drive home alone, but it gave me time to reflect on everything that was happening in our family and how I would make the most of my five days at home.

When I walked through the door of our home, it was a strange feeling. The whole house looked different. Nothing had been done to it, but it had been a month since I'd been there, and things seemed to have changed. It made me think about how our lives had also changed and would probably never be quite the same.

I decided to take both my daughters out and spend one day of just "girl time," doing nothing but shopping, eating, and laughing together. We all needed to be reminded that we can still laugh and enjoy life. So I took Stacey out of school for the day and picked Kayla up and went shopping. What a great time to just be girls and have fun.

Posted October 1, 2008 by Ranae

I know Randy said he was going to type something at noon, but I just had to share what I read this morning because it encouraged me so much that I wanted to encourage you all as well.

First Peter 1:3-9: "Praise be to the God and Father of our Lord Jesus Christ! In his great mercy He has given us new birth into a living hope through the resurrection of Jesus Christ from the dead…who through faith are shielded by God's power until the coming of the salvation that is ready to be revealed in the last time. In this you greatly rejoice, though now for a little while you may have had to suffer grief in all kinds of trials. These have come so that your faith…may be proved genuine and may result in praise…"

It's a lot but worth the read! We don't serve a dead King. He is very much alive and giving us that living hope, and it's God's power that shields us even though we suffer trials.

It's been wonderful to be home with Tony, Kayla, and Stacey. This morning I was missing the normalcy of life, and then God directed me to this passage. Does He care or what? It says that even though we've never seen Him, we love Him and believe in Him, which fills us with inexpressible and glorious joy. How true!!

Randy spent the week in Chicago with Isaiah, and it was good for him to see Isaiah working hard at his therapies, yet also see the continued struggles he is having.

Posted October 2, 2008 by Randy

As we go through this journey in our lives, I was thinking about how we can be so strong and courageous at times only to turn around and be so weak. I think that people don't always realize Isaiah's struggles yet during this trial in his life. Every day he attacks each therapy with ambition and strength. But at times we can tell he is frustrated. In PT he jumps all over, but when it is time to work on his cognitive skills, it is so hard for him. He has times when he can't tell the differences between colors or shapes. Then the next time he will spit them out in complete sentences with great confidence.

Isaiah did well again today with all the therapies, especially speech. It is hard at times to watch him. The kid that was an A student, trying to do simple tasks with math problems or reading. But again, with the physical therapy he excels. I did have a bit of a breakdown yesterday in speech when Isaiah sang his favorite song, "Strong Tower." We also sang "Holy, Holy" by Kutless, and it made me shed a few tears as I thought, "Here he was having trouble speaking sentences, but he could sing out praises to God with lifted arms and clenched fists."

Wow! Back at the Ronald McDonald House I have been reading a short devotional by Max Lucado on Psalm 23. Last night he wrote about God's grace to us and that He understands where we are because He has been there. He extends His grace to us to help us in our times of need.

Hebrews 4:15-16 were used as a reference: "For we do not have a high priest who is unable to sympathize with our weakness, but we have One who has been tempted in every way--just as we are--yet was without sin. Let us then approach the throne of grace with confidence, so that we may receive mercy and find grace to help us in our time of need."

I think the last part is so important. We are to approach the throne with confidence because Christ is with us. He is in control and willing to help ease our pain if we are only willing to turn to Him. Jesus WILL help us in our times of need. We continually tell Isaiah to ask God to help him when he feels down and show God's love through him.

Posted October 5, 2008 by Ranae

My week at home was gone way too fast! After I dropped Stacey off at 6:00 a.m. volleyball practice, I went home and sat on her bed. I cried because I knew it was going to be a while before I would be home with her again. As I prayed for her, God brought me such comfort in knowing that this time would go fast and also that He is doing a work in her life too! Then I went down to the kitchen and ate some chocolate! It helps!!

Coming back to Chicago was a long drive, but when I walked into Isaiah's room and saw Randy and Isaiah, it was so uplifting! I couldn't believe in one week how well his walking and talking had improved. We just had a great time together and enjoyed the visitors!

I'm going to bed early tonight, so this will be short, but as I reflected on this past week and how great it was to be home, how hard it was to leave, and then how happy I was to see the guys, it made me think of the verses in Habakkuk 3:17-18: "Though the fig tree does not bud and there are no grapes on the vine...yet I will rejoice in the LORD, I will be joyful in God my Savior.

Even though things don't go according to how I think they should go, or they take a different turn than I expected, all these things are minor compared to my relationship with Christ. He is my strength. I am a weakling.

Love you all and thank you for flooding heaven with prayers for Isaiah.

Isaiah was a very determined young man. Each day we could see him giving it his all in each of his therapies. I believe his football workouts had given him the self-motivation to push harder and give more than 100% to everything, and it was paying off. He began to use the stairs, with help, and his balance continually improved.

By this time he was on solid food and was receiving enough calories from his food so that his G-tube could come out. Since this was all new to me, I wasn't sure how this was going to take place. The tube went directly through the front of his abdomen all the way through to his stomach. On the inside of his stomach was a small balloon which was inflated to keep the tube from coming out.

Posted October 6, 2008 by Ranae

"Oh, LORD!" These were the words out of Isaiah's mouth when the doctor pulled out his G-tube today. No kidding! They just deflated the air sack inside his stomach with a syringe and then yanked out the tube. I was surprised that Isaiah didn't yell. He only gave a heavy sigh, and the look on his face said, "Holy cow that hurt!" He looked at me and all he said was, "Oh, LORD! That was hard!" This was a step in the road to recovery and another step closer to going home. It will take a few days to heal, but he is doing fine with a little Tylenol.

He had a great day in PT and took two flights of stairs, up and down, placing each foot on the next step, both ways! They also had him stand on a platform that was cut in a moon shape on the bottom to help him improve his balance. While he stood on the platform, he had to shoot baskets. He fell of a couple times but recovered on his own, getting his balance before getting back on.

He has made plenty of gains in OT as well. He can pretty much bathe himself with very little assistance and dresses himself with only some help in tying his shoes.

During SPT today, she worked to get him to recognize objects and to use a sentence to answer questions. He did an excellent job at that. He read words that she wrote down, like helicopter, airplane, train, traffic light, and more. His attention span has really increased, so he is able to stay with a project for a longer period of time.

I want to thank his CORE group from Waverly-Shell Rock High for the care package. He beat me twice in the football toss game today, and that was using his right hand.

He was thrilled when he called Cody this afternoon and found out that he was at football practice, so he got to talk to coach and the rest of the team. His face was glowing and his smile huge from being able to talk to you guys!

Isaiah finally was able to wash his own face and brush his own teeth. Although you and I take these things for granted, he had to relearn all of it. It was like watching a baby learn how to do everything, only in fast-forward speed. He was proud of each accomplishment and each one made him all the more determined.

Up to this point, Isaiah had been sleeping in a tent bed which zipped from the outside so the patient couldn't get out of bed or fall out of bed and get hurt. It gave me peace of mind knowing that when I left for the night, Isaiah was safely tucked in and would not fall out and hurt himself. By mid-October, Isaiah's stamina was better, and he was able to stay up later, so that meant I was getting back to the house later. I really hated leaving him because he was more aware that I left in the evenings.

Posted October 8, 2008 by Ranae

Psalm 147: "Praise the LORD. How good it is to sing praises to our God, how pleasant and fitting to praise Him. He heals the broken hearted and binds up their wounds."

I was encouraged by these words this morning since we had a tough evening last night. Isaiah is becoming more aware of his limitations and didn't want to come in from outside. When I asked him if he wanted to call someone, he said, "No, I can't say...words...right." He is aware that the words don't come out like he wants, and he didn't want me to leave for the evening. So I stayed until he went to sleep and prayed God would help him and encourage him to keep on going.

This morning he was in a better mood and worked hard at all the therapies. His balance has improved, and he had to walk, stop, pick up a ball by bending at the knees, and then stand up with it. He also got to play Wii with Mike, and he used his right hand every time. It was fun to see him enjoying it, and he did pretty well.

Also this morning, the doctors discussed his attention span and how it has improved, so they are going to back him off his Amantadine to see how he does. If it doesn't go well, they will try to place him on Ritalin. I'm concerned about all the potential side effects of these drugs. I'm open to use them if needed but would rather try without them.

Posted October 9, 2008 by Ranae

Isaiah had a great day! He started off with PT, and they pushed him to try harder at balancing. Today he almost ran down the hallway, and when the PT therapist said, "Stop!" he had to stop without taking a step. Mike also had him sit on an exercise ball and catch a smaller ball while keeping his balance. He only fell off once but recovered smoothly. I've been cleared to walk him in the hallways, so we do this every chance we get so it will build his stamina and walking confidence.

He was very talkative with his tutor today. He explained about the calf he caught at the fair a few years ago and became quite expressive, even though not all the words came out clearly. Nevertheless, he was excited when talking about it. He has become quite the funny guy lately too. He laughs a lot and was joking with another patient when they were playing a game together. It is such a blessing to see this.

He has a long way to go yet in his speaking and in his use of words, but I prayed with him tonight before he went to sleep. I thought about how far he has come and how blessed we are to even have him here with us. I know this was God reminding me that He is still walking this path with us and comforting me that He has a plan for Isaiah. I'm so thankful and grateful.

I know God does not always answer prayers the way people think He should, and when I think about what he has done for Isaiah already, I know it is an undeserved blessing he has granted our family. It has been a "stretching" experience for all of us, but we know when we come through on the other side of it, we will be more mature people as a result.

The only medicine Isaiah is on now is a half dose of Amantadine. That's it. No Propanelol or anything! Praise God for that! We decided to celebrate his accomplishments by taking up a new friend on her offer to take us to the Hershey Store downtown. It was wonderful!!

Finally the date was set for Isaiah's departure! On November 7, 2008, Isaiah would be discharged from inpatient rehab! With only a few weeks left, there was much to accomplish and "pass" in order to be released.

About two weeks before our impending return home, I came into

Isaiah's room at about 6:30 a.m. He was sitting up in his bed just looking around. A wide smile spread across his face when he saw me, and he inched closer to the corner of the tent. He then tried to show me how I should unzip the zipper to the tent about three inches down. I asked him why he wanted me to do that, but he couldn't find the words to explain, so I did as he showed me. It turns out that he had contemplated all night how he was going to escape his "tent prison." To my surprise, he swiftly put his fingers through the three-inch opening and proceeded to unzip the whole thing!

When Dr. Sisung came in for rounds that morning, I told him what Isaiah had asked and done, and he thought it was probably time for him to be out of the tent. The look on Isaiah's face was one of great relief.

That day was the beginning of another significant change. Although Isaiah still could only speak in two-to-three-word sentences, he was better able to get his point across by gesturing or pointing at objects and making different expressive sounds. He also clearly understood that day what had happened to him as he asked me in broken English why we were in Chicago. He wondered if he had crashed his motorcycle and thought that if we called Dad, he could get here in a few hours, and we could all go home.

Months later, he was better able to explain his thinking that day. He told us he had awakened during the night and thought he had been taken prisoner. He remembered going to bed in his own room only to wake up in this "prison." He couldn't see anyone, and he thought America had been taken over by another country and that he was a prisoner in a foreign land. When I walked into the room, he was relieved to see me and learn that he indeed was not a prisoner. I felt badly I had not been there to comfort him when he "awoke". I'm not sure how long he sat there waiting but I knew something had definitely changed in him because he was more inquisitive.

We had two weeks left of therapy, but he just wanted to go home, so I decided to make a chart for him so he could mark off the days. We marked off each day, but they simply were not going quickly enough for him. He would call Randy and Tony several times a day, asking them to come to Chicago and get us. He now realized he was missing his junior year of high school, and he wanted to get back to school for the third quarter. He was so determined that he "told" everyone by holding up three fingers that third quarter was his goal and nothing was going to stop him.

I gave up the room at the Ronald McDonald House and slept in the chair in his room. Now that Isaiah was out of the tent, I didn't feel comfortable leaving him alone. I knew he might try to get out of bed, and I didn't want him falling and hitting his head. This ended up being my dilemma for quite some time, always wanting to be there for him in case he needed me.

About a week before we were to go home, Isaiah was walking so much better that he decided he wasn't going to sit in the wheelchair any longer. He walked to each of his therapies. It took him longer to get places, but that didn't matter to him. He was walking and there was no going back to that chair for him!

Jack and Isaiah had become friends, and Jack's mom asked if we would like to walk down to the movie theater with them. We thought it would be fun for the guys to have that kind of normalcy in their lives again. The theater was five or six blocks away, and our plan was to push them in their wheelchairs. However, Isaiah quickly let me know he was not getting back in that chair! I thought how much easier and faster it would be if I pushed him in the wheelchair, but I knew his mind was made up. He was going to walk it no matter how much slower it would be. And he did!

Back home, Randy was still trying to keep things going with Stacey and work and housekeeping. When an event like this happens, people have a tendency to forget that life goes on for the rest of the family. They were trying to deal with the everyday tasks that still needed doing, many of which I had been responsible for.

With me being in Chicago I had to give up my bi-weekly cleaning job, and as a photographer, I had to drop all my clients for senior portraits. It was more than a year after being home before I was able to take appointments again. I totally gave up the cleaning job as I was going to be the full time chauffeur for Isaiah to all his appointments. This meant Randy had to work hard to maintain his job and also added more responsibilities at home. He was working, trying to make it to Stacey's volleyball games after school, doing laundry and cooking meals. Stacey said she ate a lot of corn dogs and chicken nuggets—things she could quickly heat up in the microwave. All of this prompted Randy's next post.

Posted October 15, 2008 by Randy

Okay, this is the time that we--or I--have to confess that I need Ranae to guide me in the right direction as a man. I'm like 0 for 2 this week in being at the right place at the right time. Monday was a volleyball game with Parkersburg. No problem. Since the high school had been demolished by a tornado that spring, I figured the game was at Aplington at 5:00 p.m. like all the rest of the freshman games. I walked in with confidence that the game had just started. Wrong! As the "social directors" of the other girls informed me, it started at 4:30. I only got in on the last half of game three.

Then came Tuesday night--parents' night, volleyball, home game. Grandma Krull was in town, so I picked her up to go to the games. I watched the ninth grade girls play. Great game girls! Two and out! They decided to play a few extra games...great! I watched, but Stacey was also watching... from the bench. So I asked Grandma if she wanted to see the display they had for Isaiah in the junior hallway, and we took off.

We ran into a wonderful teacher who showed us the way, and we spent some time looking at the display and talking about Isaiah. Time to get back, but we wanted to hit the concession stand first. Plenty of time---or so I thought.

"Introduction of the freshman players, and would their parents please stand as their names are called." And where is Randy?? Chewing down a pork burger. Sorry Stacey!

She forgave me, but I'm still wondering what it's going to cost me?! Yes, if I'd had Ranae by my side, this never would have happened. I admit it. Two days in a row I needed her here to point me in the right direction.

Oh, and I also found out you cannot leave shirts in the dryer overnight. Not unless you like to iron. So now what? I DON'T IRON! The solution? Washing and drying them all over again.

Okay, and I'm bad, but I just didn't like cooking in those pans. So another thing I found out is that if I didn't like something in the house, this was a good time to toss it out!

I know this whole blog was not very spiritual. Just wanted you to know I miss Ranae and Isaiah.

These are only a few of the behind-the-scenes things that can happen to families going through crisis. Simple, everyday tasks that get thrown into the mix can cause problems. Randy actually did throw away one of my pans, but I wasn't too upset since it was in poor shape anyway! What did bother me, even though I knew I was badly needed in Chicago, was the helpless feeling of being so far away from the rest of my family. I wasn't there to help Randy with all the daily housekeeping tasks and scheduling dilemmas. I wasn't there to greet Stacey with "How did high school go for you today?" or to attend those volleyball games. At the same time, they were torn between carrying on with life at home and wanting to be in Chicago with Isaiah and me.

When tragedies come, they affect the whole family, who not only must mentally, physically, and emotionally deal with the tragedy itself, but also must try to keep up with some sort of normal life as well. And, with young teens, they're old enough to realize the magnitude of the tragedy, but too young to have good coping skills.

We were definitely learning as we went, and if something were to happen again, I know there are a few things I would do differently. In particular, I now realize it may be necessary to ask family or friends to step in and help, especially as far as any younger siblings are concerned. They are hurting, but they are trying to be strong for the rest of the family while still dealing with their own fears, changes in family dynamics, and mundane chores and school work. They are not only missing Mom or Dad, but are also worried about and missing their injured brother or sister. Wherever my family went--church, grocery store, anywhere--the first questions asked were "How is Isaiah doing? How is Ranae holding up?" Rarely, if ever, did anyone follow those with "And how are the rest of the kids handling all of this? Is there anything we can do for them?"

It's one of the lessons I've had to learn. My other children were suffering. They put on brave faces, but troubling questions were brewing behind those faces. *How could God let this happen to our brother? He always stood up for what he believed, so why would God punish him this way?* These were huge questions that stormed through their minds, and yet they weren't discussing them with anyone because they felt guilty for questioning God. These were all real emotions and fears, but I was not seeing what was going on with them because I was consumed with making sure Isaiah was getting the help he needed.

A crisis like this can cause a family tremendous stress. Marriages have been known to fail under it; children can become withdrawn and depressed; angry and aggressive. It may be difficult for those outside of the crisis to realize how the family is dealing with it. Even though it has been three years since Isaiah's accident, it continues to have its effects on his brother and sisters. He is not the same, and they are still trying to deal with both the changes in him and the changes within the family.

If there is something good that has come from all of this, it is that each of us is now more empathetic towards families in crisis. Because of what our family has been through, we are better able to respond to whatever painful trial another family might be facing. I have seen it mature the other members of my family.

As the time approached to come home, Isaiah had to prove to the OT that he could shower on his own. He was still very modest about showing any part of his body to any female, and the thought of stripping down and showering in front of her was a bit more than he could take. Not only did he have to do it in front of her, but she happened to have a female intern working with her at the time.

The day of the big test, Isaiah kept getting out of his chair, walking to the door and looking down the hallway. He paced back and forth, waiting for these two women to come into the room. I told him not to worry about it; that they had done this many times before, but that did little to comfort him.

When they finally arrived in the room, they asked if he was ready, and then all three of them walked into the bathroom. Suddenly, Isaiah turned around, walked out the door and closed it behind him. Christy, the OT, laughed as she came out of the bathroom. She said she had never had anyone try to lock her in the bathroom before! It was obviously time for a compromise—they allowed Isaiah to keep his gym shorts on while he showered. Everyone was happy and relieved when he passed this test!

I think the thing that impressed me the most through all of this was Isaiah's attitude and sense of humor. While Randy was there, he said the physical therapist had Isaiah walk down the hallway at a quick pace. When they reached the end of the hall, Isaiah dropped to the floor and began rubbing his legs. Randy asked him what was wrong, but Isaiah only grimaced and kept massaging his legs. The therapist hurried over to see what the problem was and then a wide smile crossed Isaiah's face. FAKER!! Randy realized Isaiah was joking around with them. This was just the first of many jokes Isaiah would try to play on his therapists!

This new personality was starting to emerge, and I didn't know if it would continue or if it was just a phase brain-injured patients experienced. He normally was quiet, so this was totally out of character. Of course, his father was known to have a dry sense of humor and could tease along with the best of them. Maybe this was a trait the two of them would now share in common even as other former bonds might change.

Posted October 26, 2008 by Randy

Today was the opening of pheasant-hunting season, a day Isaiah, Tony, and I would have normally traveled to Buffalo Center to participate in. Grandma would have made us a big breakfast, and we'd have been off to our favorite hunting grounds. The last three years had been especially great, and we had our limits by early afternoon. Then we would go back to town for another feast, with Grandma making sure we cleaned our plates, a task Isaiah was very good at completing.

Not this year. I just couldn't bring myself to get out the shotgun yet. This event had become very special to me over the years, something the boys and I could do and have a lot of fun doing.

I think my way of dealing with tough times is just to keep busy, and that's what I did today. I did get a lot done in preparation for winter, making sheds ready for storage and just good old cleanup. I know I could have called a few people to help, but I simply needed the day for myself. Instead of hunting, I'm staying in Shell Rock this weekend.

As Ranae stated in her update, Friday night was hard. As Isaiah is getting stronger and more aware, he thinks he is ready to move on. Friday night he was determined to come home, pleading with me to bring the car and pick him and mom up and take them home.

Phone calls like that and days like today bring thoughts of Why did this have to happen? I was flipping through my Bible tonight and came across a note I had put down in one of the blank pages. It read…"It is not my responsibility to understand God and how He works in our lives, but to obey Him." This statement was referring to Judges 7 and the story of Gideon and his battle against the Midianites.

In this story, Gideon was heading into battle with 32,000 men, and God basically told him it was too many. Through a series of events, God narrowed the army down to a mere 300 men to fight the battle. (Now that is a greater reduction than the stock market dropping!) I would think that these men may have even been depressed over the odds against them. But God told them to trust Him and not the odds, and He would deliver the victory.

Hebrews 11:1: "Faith is being sure of what we hope for and certain of what we do not see." These men, including Gideon, had a lesson not on understanding but on believing. So also, God brought me back around again by saying, "Trust me. Have faith in me."

I would invite you to read Gideon's story in the Bible and check out the battle. Like Gideon, I do not understand God's plan, and that can be hard for a guy since we like to fix everything. But I know I need to trust God's plan for Isaiah and my family. I guess we all have to look at ourselves at times and ask ourselves what we trust in. Material things? The stock market? My marriage? Me, myself and I? Are we even looking in the right place?

Revelations 3:19-20: "Those whom I love I rebuke and discipline. So be earnest and repent. Here I am. I stand at the door and knock. If anyone hears my voice and opens the door, I will come in and eat with him and he with Me." Jesus in inviting us into fellowship with Him, but we have to respond and open the door. It's kind of like getting a cell phone call. We usually see who it's from before we answer it. The people we don't want to talk to we just ignore. But Jesus is our friend and a friend worth taking the call from. Thank you, Jesus, for your many "calls" as presented in your Word, the Bible, and often just when we need them.

I would invite you to answer the phone the next time He calls. By the way, He is always calling for you!

The air was cooling off, and our trips to Navy Pier were becoming fewer because it was much cooler walking down there. The trees in front of and around the rehab had turned to beautiful shades of red, yellow, orange, and purple. As I looked out Isaiah's window and across Lake Michigan, I realized another season was approaching. It had felt like only days since our first experience in Chicago, the experience of being in such a big city and not knowing our way around. Now, looking out the fifth floor window, I had come to know my way around very well and could go anywhere within ten blocks and know exactly where I was. It's strange how we adapt to different surroundings.

I missed going to church. It had been three months since I was able to attend our church back home. Now I was in this huge city and wanted to go to church. But where? I decided to go online and see what churches were available downtown and found out there was a branch of Willow Creek just two miles from the rehab. I knew this was too far for Isaiah to walk, but we could take a cab! He was able to walk better and was able to sit through a service, and I thought he might enjoy listening to some live worship music instead of his tapes. Besides, we didn't have any visitors coming that weekend, and Sunday would get to be long just walking around the rehab.

Posted October 27, 2008 by Ranae

Isaiah and I got to go to church at the downtown location of Willow Creek Church on Sunday. We walked down to Michigan Avenue and took a taxicab from there. It took Isaiah a bit to get into the cab, but he made it! The Auditorium Theatre is a beautiful building and a landmark in Chicago.

The worship was wonderful! Isaiah kept smiling at me and sang along with all the songs.

Wouldn't you know it? The message was about how youth of our culture can be an influence. It was taken from 2Chronicles about Josiah when he became king at the age of 8 and how he walked in the steps of his father, David. By the age of 16, he was seeking after God wholeheartedly, and at 20 he was ridding the country of all the idols.

Sometimes we tend to underestimate what our youth are capable of doing. It was just a good reminder to me that we are responsible to train and teach these young people how to love God and live for Him and learn to obey His voice. It can be overwhelming at times, but God gives us what we need when we need it, and He is invested in them even greater than we are.

Today was a day of more improvements for Isaiah. In PT he worked on doing the stairs with more ease going up and down. He also pushed himself more than what his therapist expected of him. He was to hold in a crunch position for one minute, but Isaiah decided to hold it for an extra forty seconds just to push himself!

When he got back to the room, he kept jogging from one end to the other and touching the walls to give himself more exercise! You just have to love the determination!

OT had him carving out a pumpkin. Using his right hand, he had to pull out all the seeds and gunk from inside the pumpkin. Then he got to carve it out. It is difficult for him to use his right hand and very slow, but they kept pushing him to continue to use it.

He had a hard workout in SPT today, but his therapist said he did a wonderful job. He still needs some cuing with the first sound on words, but today she let him struggle a bit to try to find the right words on his own, and he really did well. He is working on categorizing words, which helps him find the right words to get across his ideas.

He is really counting down the days until he gets to come home. I'm excited, and yet, at the same time, I know this will be a big adjustment as well because he will not be able to do all the things I know he is going to want to do. He won't be able to be left alone, and it will be some time before he can drive and go to school. As he continues to heal and understand things better, he is going to want to do all these things but will not be allowed to do so until it is safe for him.

Posted October 31, 2008 at 10:27 p.m. by Ranae

The days are counting down. The release date of November 7 can't come quickly enough. The last two days have been fun with Isaiah and seeing the progress he has made. It is really amazing, and the biggest change has been with his mind. In working on school work sheets, he is remembering equations and is able to spell out our names and his address.

As we walk around the center, we sometimes hear other patients refusing to do something, but you will never hear that from Isaiah. He is smart enough to know how to answer people's questions with short answers and cover his difficulties at times, but he also knows the people who won't let him get by that easily.

Today I was going through Isaiah's care pages with some of the staff and showing them Isaiah's story. It became clear once again how blessed I am to have my son back. I was going through the pictures, and Isaiah asked a lot of questions about his condition back in Iowa City and how we got to Chicago. He kept saying, "Look at me now!"

All day today he was in a very jolly mood and full of jokes. But the best was in OT. We had gotten back from walking the hallways, and I had made a comment that he might be really tired from all the pool therapy and walking six floors. As we were just about ready to end the session, Isaiah said his legs were feeling weird, and he kept slapping them as if trying to wake them up. I asked if they were tingling or hurt. We had him try to stand up, and he fell back into the chair. The therapist and I looked at each other with a "Now what?" glance. Then Isaiah stood up, grinned, and apologized for the tease.

He is SO ready to come home!

Even though Isaiah realized he had been in a terrible accident and would still have a long road of recovery, he maintained a very positive and grateful attitude. He was just thankful to be alive and recognized that each day was a gift.

Randy, Isaiah, and I were passing through the hallways, saying our goodbyes to the many families we had come to know. It was difficult knowing many had a long road yet and others were close to their own goal of leaving the inpatient rehab. As we checked out at the front desk and I watched Isaiah pass through the revolving doors it dawned on me that he was leaving the building, walking on his own accord. Yes, like that verse God had given me back in Iowa City, Isaiah was walking. God had kept His promise!

Chapter Eight
Coming Home

*I*t was partially snowing, partially raining, but that didn't matter. We were on our way home!! The five-hour drive could not go fast enough for me. It had been three-and-a-half long months away with only a few days here and there to spend at home with my other children, and this was going to be a wonderful homecoming!

It was Friday, and a big welcome home party was planned for that Sunday afternoon at the public library. Stacey had called me that morning, wondering if she could stay home from school. She was in the process of working on a DVD for Isaiah and wanted to finish it before he got home. Okay, I had gotten soft—I let her stay home from school. Besides, I knew she wanted to be there when we pulled into the drive.

Isaiah beamed from ear to ear as we drove onto our acreage. It seemed that being in familiar surroundings again was helping jog his memory, and it was fun to see his siblings there to greet him.

After all the hugs and kisses, we went into the house to see a big *Welcome Home Isaiah* banner hanging in the doorway. Home never felt so good, and it was wonderful to have our entire family together there again. This whole experience had made each of us search our own souls and realize how precious life is. We no longer would take each other for granted, and for me, no one would ever get out the door again without a hug and kiss. No regrets.

Isaiah took his time walking around the house and taking it all in. He noticed Stacey had a new CD player in her room, and he checked out everything in his own room.

One of the accommodations we had to have for his return was an alarm on his bedroom door which would sound if he tried to leave his room during the night. We have a flight of fourteen stair steps to get down to the main floor, and the doctors were concerned that Isaiah might fall down them. Isaiah wasn't excited about the alarm, but he didn't protest.

I couldn't sleep very well that night, wondering if he would try to get up or not. I also wondered what thoughts were going through his head as he lay in his own room and considered how much his life had changed. He would have to be very careful to protect his head and would no longer be able to participate in contact sports. How would his friends respond to him now? What would school look like now? So many questions. How could I even doubt what God would do? I had seen Him do so much already, and yet here I lay, worrying about the upcoming days. Shame on me! It reminded me how quickly I had forgotten what God had done, just like the Israelites back in the land of Canaan. They had seen the many miracles God performed in Egypt, and yet they quickly turned to idols once they reached Mt. Sinai. I was no different, and I asked my LORD Jesus to help my wavering faith.

Just to show me that He wasn't finished with Isaiah yet, I woke the next morning to a knocking sound. It was Isaiah across the hall, knocking from the inside of his own door. I went to his door, unhooked the alarm, and opened it. Isaiah was standing there, waiting for us to come. He didn't want to wake us up by setting off an alarm, so instead he knocked to get our attention! This may seem small, but to me it was a sign that Isaiah was thinking things through and "getting it" and he would be okay.

Sunday afternoon we walked into the library to find many family and friends there, anxious to see Isaiah. Although, he still had difficulty with his words, Isaiah was so excited to see everyone and shake hands to show his gratefulness for all the prayers for his recovery. We showed the DVD Stacey had put together and it was very powerful. We had to make extra copies for family members and friends as they wanted to use it to share with others they knew going through their own struggles.

It was still difficult for Isaiah to get words out correctly to explain what he was thinking, but he became quite good at explaining what things *did* in order to help us understand what he was talking about. For example, Stacey was vacuuming the floor, and he couldn't remember what the machine was called, so he described it as the *floor sucker*. He was very excited about Jesus returning to the earth to rapture up all believers, but since he couldn't remember the word *rapture*, he would say *getting sucked up*. We tried to help him a little by giving him the first sounds of words he was trying to say, but we wanted him to continue to work on finding the words himself.

Probably one of the hardest things to adjust to was the change in his personality. He had always been more on the quiet side, but now he was very open to talk about anything and everything. This was hard because we all kept expecting the old Isaiah to return. Even now, three years later, I think we are finally realizing that a part of the old Isaiah is gone, and this is who he is now.

We were home, and yet I found it more difficult to cope. Life was moving forward at the same rapid pace it was before the accident happened. Stacey had basketball games and practice. Tony had just purchased his first home and would be needing help with painting, and people started calling me to take senior pictures. Then there were still the daily tasks like washing clothes and making meals. Plus, since I had been gone for over three months, I was trying to catch up with friends and family.

The difference was now, I had a disabled child to help. That's right--a disabled child who needed me to take him to therapy each day. Never, did I ever think I would be in such a position, and yet this is where Jesus had placed me. One of the hardest parts of being back home was dealing with all the questions people had about Isaiah. Every brain injury is different yet challenging. Most people didn't realize what is involved when it comes to dealing with a person who has a brain injury.

I think family and friends expected Isaiah to be the same person, and he wasn't. He was much more outspoken, especially about his faith.

As I watched him talking with people, I could see them blowing off what he was saying as if he didn't know what was going on. This was very difficult to watch because I knew Isaiah was just adamant about others coming to know Christ. He didn't want anyone to pass from this life into eternity without having a personal relationship with Jesus. He knew how quickly his life could have been taken, and this gave him more motivation to share with others about where they stood with Christ. The problem was, he couldn't always get the point across as well as he wanted to because of his difficulty in word recall. For some, his efforts were tolerated. For others, they were pitied or even ignored. And yet, Isaiah's whole attitude was so positive that it was an encouragement to me. He would smile at me and say, "I shouldn't be here, so every day is a gift!"

I was finally beginning to allow myself to "feel" all the emotions that had been bottled up for the past three months. My survival mode was slowly lifting, and little by little I was able to let go of all the fears, anxieties, and hurts. I would cry at seemingly small things, but it felt good to let it out. This would be the norm for me over several months as I allowed myself to grieve a little for what we had lost--our old Isaiah--and began to get to know the new Isaiah.

Our next step was to meet with the school to set up an IEP (Individualized Education Plan) for Isaiah. At the beginning, I didn't even know what that was or what it involved. I was so far out of my comfort zone, but I knew an IEP was needed to help Isaiah get back to school.

Our high school's staff did a wonderful job of walking us through what they would do to help Isaiah and our family so that Isaiah could meet his goal of getting back to school by the third quarter. We would need to meet with them once a month since Isaiah continued to improve, and his IEP would need to be updated more frequently than the usual once a year.

During our meetings, we had a speech therapist, occupational therapist, and an Area Education Consultant present. They were so helpful at directing us in what assistive technology would help Isaiah in the classroom. We purchased a laptop computer for him to take to classes with him with programs that would read scanned-in texts to him.

To help him write, he had Dragon Naturally Speaking. This "dragon" was programmed to recognize his voice. He would put on earphones with a mic attached. Then, as he talked, it would type whatever he said. It was fairly accurate on most words. Only occasionally would he have to retype a word. This was so helpful since Isaiah was having difficulty writing with his right-hand spasticity.

Another piece of technology that became very helpful was the use of a Flip camera. He was allowed to video the teachers' lectures and any notes written on the board, and when he came home, we would download them to our computer. He could listen to the lecture again to help him recall the new information the teacher had presented.

Besides getting ready to start school again, we needed to set up a schedule for daily outpatient therapy. We only were home a few days when Isaiah began his outpatient therapy routine at Covenant Medical Center in Waterloo, Iowa. We drove thirty miles a day to Covenant for speech, occupational, and physical therapies. Although this was not as intense as the therapy he'd had in Chicago, it still wore him out, and he was usually sleeping by seven or seven-thirty each night.

Starting after Thanksgiving, our initial routine was to drive to therapy each morning and then drive back to Waverly to the high school to meet with the special education teacher after the school day was done. Isaiah was not able to read at all and had a difficult time following directions and remembering the names of people and places. It was difficult to watch this former straight-A student who had once taken advanced placement classes now struggle to sound out words.

It was also difficult for our daughter Stacey. Her big brother had gone from a confident football player to someone who couldn't walk very well, couldn't talk very clearly, and had a hard time socially with his friends. To see him always trying to wrestle the other boys to prove how strong he still was often embarrassed her. Her life had also changed, and now she was learning to deal with all the changes in our family. She was grateful to have Isaiah alive and home, but at the same time, he was not the same brother she had once known. Things were different, and her friends were not sure what to say to her. They never asked her anything about Isaiah because they didn't want her to cry, and they weren't exactly sure what *to* say.

Music played an important role for Stacey as well. The DVD she put together using all the pictures we had taken of Isaiah's accident included three very powerful songs. As the pictures scrolled through, the songs "Strong Tower," "Praise You in This Storm," and "IN ME" play in the background as viewers watch the progression of Isaiah's initial days in ICU to his recovery in Chicago. There can be a lot of healing power in music, and this was one way Stacey could help put her feelings into a creative memory of what had happened.

Stacey was not the only sibling to have a life change. Tony had continued to see Bailey, the young nurse from Iowa City who had taken care of Isaiah the second day in the PICU. They had made many trips back and forth, and he had met her family. Since I had been gone for three months, I hadn't realized how serious they had become, but it was now very evident that Bailey might be a soul mate for Tony.

That Christmas was an extra special one since we had everyone there. Isaiah was so excited to discover that Tony had found someone he loved and that he had played a part in their meeting each other. He took full credit for lining up his older brother! Kayla and her boyfriend David were there, and it was just a wonderful blessing to celebrate the birth of our Lord and Savior Jesus Christ all together as a family.

The high school's third quarter started shortly after Christmas, and Isaiah was signed up for two classes: math and English. Normally, Isaiah would have been in Algebra 2, but now he would have a parapro-fessional with him in a General Math classroom where they would try to jumpstart his natural math ability. English would be another story. In one way or another, his brain injury had affected his ability to read, write, and speak.

At our first IEP meeting, Mr. Winter, our high school principal, had suggested a retired English teacher to work with him on his English credit. She was there and was quite excited to help this young man regain her language skills. I didn't know her since none of my children had ever had her for a class. She was a very tall, blonde woman with a jovial personality, and she was willing to work with Isaiah one-on-one for two periods every morning. She also would help reinforce the exercises his speech therapist and his occupational therapist brought to their classroom each month.

I don't know how else to say it, but she was a God-send! God knew who Isaiah would need to help him get back into the school mode, and she was just the right fit. Since she had taken early retirement the summer before, she had the time to prepare an individual lesson for Isaiah, and not only that, she took a personal interest in him as well. He was her student, and she was his. She learned what interested him and made that part of the lesson plans. They hit it off from the start!

Shortly after they started working together, it was Winterfest at the high school, and Isaiah wanted to dress like Mrs. Whitney on the week's look-alike day. We borrowed a blond wig from some friends, and I made a lanyard and a homemade copy of her identity badge for Isaiah to wear. Mrs. Whitney was unaware of this plan but was pleasantly surprised and caught on immediately when she saw the blond wig and lanyard.

As he was leaving his math class that morning, another math teacher told him he'd better hurry to get to his next class. He flipped his blond hair back and quickly replied, "I don't have to. I'm retired!" This drew a laugh from the teacher who was also astonished at the change in his personality. He had always been very quiet before and did not share a lot with anyone. Now he loved to joke around and make others laugh.

Before the accident, Isaiah had been basically alone in the back room of our church directing the shots for the camera people out in the sanctuary. Now he decided he didn't want to do that anymore. He wanted to be out greeting people as they came in the doors of the church. This just wasn't the same guy who had preferred the back room to the front door!

Mrs. Whitney didn't know Isaiah before the accident, so she couldn't make this kind of comparison in his personality. But she was also intrigued when she heard about his reply to the math teacher. She knew that kind of wit meant there was a definite intelligence there that needed nurturing, and it motivated her even more to try and unlock it.

From his outward appearance, Isaiah looks just like he did before the accident. But now his speech is not as easy to understand, and his processing speed is slow. I compare it to the internet. Those who have dial-up will totally understand what I'm talking about when I say it is VERY slow to get connected and browse the web, while high-speed internet may take only seconds to do both. When information comes into Isaiah's brain, it takes longer to process it; then it takes another minute or so for him to formulate an answer. He gets to the right answer, just like dial-up does, but it takes him longer.

This can be frustrating for people listening to him, especially when he's on the phone. I might ask him a question, and it might take him a minute to answer me. I've had people ask if he is still on the line, and they don't always understand the time it takes for him to absorb information and formulate an answer before he can reply. Our brains are miraculously made, but when they are "broken," it can affect many of the other parts of the body. To the general public who is used to a quick reply, it is difficult to have patience with someone with a brain injury.

I have been saddened at times to see how some people respond to Isaiah. As a parent, it is hard to watch how they shy away from him, especially other teens. They just don't know how to respond to him. As he continues to heal, he is becoming better at his social skills, but it does take time. Initially, he wanted to arm wrestle everyone, and it became quite obvious that others were not comfortable with a 17-year-old wanting to wrestle them. So Randy and I have had to re-teach him social skills.

It seems that as each week passed, Isaiah continued to show signs of consistent improvements. His language skills improved to the point that he was able to put together sentences and was able to communicate what he needed or explain some of his difficulties with more detail. His ability to walk was also improving, and he was determined to run again.

We shared with Isaiah how we had kept care pages that updated his whole ordeal and how so many people were following his story. He was excited to hear what people had written and how people's lives had not only been impacted by our messages but also by his determination and will to get better. So, he decided it was time to enter a blog of his own.

Posted March 2, 2009 by Isaiah Krull

Hi!! 2009 years ago, who was born on the earth? It was Jesus Christ!! Do you know the passage John 3:16? "For God so loved the world, that He gave His only begotten Son, that whoever believes in Him will not perish but have everlasting life!" Oh yah!

So those who don't believe in Him won't go to Heaven but to Hell! In Hell you feel like you are on fire, but it's forever.

James 2:10: "For whoever keeps the whole law and yet stumbles at just one point is guilty of them all."

1 Corinthians6:9-10: "Do you not know that the wicked will not inherit the kingdom of God? Do not be deceived: neither the sexually immoral nor idolaters, nor adulterers nor male prostitutes nor homosexual offenders nor thieves nor the greedy nor the drunkards nor slanderers nor swindlers will inherit the kingdom of God. And that is what some of you were. But you were washed, you were sanctified, you were justified in the name of the LORD JESUS CHRIST and by the SPIRIT of our GOD!"

I was in a coma this past year, and I was pretty close to death, but thanks to God, I am not dead yet! So it's like God wanted me to say all this. So, please, let this care page text let you think about your life, because I already know that my salvation is from God!
Thanks for praying for me!! Isaiah Krull

God had done a work in Isaiah, and his compassionate heart wanted to see others come to know Jesus Christ as their personal Savior. Anyone who knows Isaiah knows he is all about making sure people have a personal relationship with Jesus. He can't always remember the right words to say, but he is very clear on asking Jesus to forgive our personal sins and come into our lives and take control over us.

As I mentioned earlier, I was studying through the book of Isaiah and found some astonishing verses.

Isaiah 45: 6-7: "I am the Lord, and there is no other. I form the light and create darkness. I bring prosperity and create disaster; I, the LORD, do all these things."

As difficult as these verses may be to wrap our minds around, they are His Word and teach us more about Him. It struck me that it's easy to accept God as forming the light and bringing prosperity, but the verse also says He forms darkness and creates disaster. How can He be a good God and do both? I've learned that He created us to be free to choose right from wrong, good or bad, sin or righteousness. We chose to sin, and all the wrong, the pain, and the suffering in this world are a result of the curse of sin.

The longer we had been home, the more time I had to recall all that had happened and all that Isaiah had lost. But then I thought about all we had gained as well. God, our heavenly Father, held us up through this most difficult time. He could have taken Isaiah from us that day, but He didn't. He allowed him to live. Yes, he had some disabilities because of his accident, but he also had a new perspective on life and what is most important here on earth.

As I read farther in the chapter, verses 9-13 go on to ask questions such as "Who made us?" God made the earth and created mankind upon it. He will raise up whom He desires because He is Sovereign over everything. He can be trusted because we know He is GOOD! So when trials come our way, we have a choice to make. We can curse God for our situation, or we can run to Him for comfort and strength. The choice is ours to make. He is ALWAYS there!

As difficult as it sometimes was to watch Isaiah struggle to improve during therapy, I was amazed and proud of how he maintained his love for Jesus and was steadfast in his love for the God who spared him. As a result, I was learning to trust God in a whole new way.

One of the issues Isaiah struggled with was his eyesight. We had not realized what he could and could not see until he had reached a point when he was able to more accurately explain to us exactly what he was seeing. We had to make a couple trips to Iowa City to a neuro-ophthalmologist. He tested his vision and discovered he had some small "blind spots" in both eyes. This had been caused by the hemorrhage he sustained during the accident. An optic nerve had been damaged, which meant this was permanent. The spots were small enough, but when Isaiah tried to read, he had trouble seeing the whole word.

Isaiah's goal was to get his driver's license back. He would have to perform several driving tests and vision tests before being cleared to drive. This was a huge prayer request because if he couldn't drive on his own, he would always have to have someone else drive for him. Losing his right to drive meant losing a lot of freedom, so this was a biggy!

After enduring all the tests, he was told his blind spots were small enough that they would not be a great detriment to his ability to drive. He would just have to learn to move his eyes and scan across the road more often than others, but he would be able to drive! The doctor looked at him and just told him to drive only where he was comfortable driving, otherwise have a friend or family member drive. This was a moment he had been waiting for. As soon as we pulled into our driveway, he jumped out, ran into the house, and grabbed his car keys. He was off to a friend's house before we made it across the yard!

Psalms: 145: 14-20a: "The Lord upholds all those who fall and lifts up all who are bowed down. The eyes of all look to You, and You give them their food at the proper time. You open Your hand and satisfy the desires of every living thing. The Lord is righteous in all His ways and loving toward all He has made. The Lord is near to all who call on Him, to all who call on Him in truth. He fulfills the desires of those who fear Him; He hears their cry and saves them. The Lord watches over all who love Him."

Isaiah picked up keyboarding as an additional class 4th quarter and was still attending outpatient therapies at Covenant in the afternoon. But on May 20, 2009, he had his last sessions in speech therapy and physical therapy. He was completely done! After ten months of hospitals and rehabs, it was a relief. But it also meant that we would have to work on things at home if he was to continue to progress.

Mrs. Whitney found out that Civics was one of the classes Isaiah would need the next year in order to graduate, so she decided to do a little advanced preparation for it. She knew he focused better if he studied something of personal interest to him, so she had him research about backseat seatbelt safety laws in Iowa.

Of course, this was something close to Isaiah's heart since he was not wearing a seatbelt in the backseat when he was in the accident. With the help of some Civics students, he put together a portfolio filled with research. Iowa required children through age ten to use some kind of backseat restraint. But that was it. Isaiah wanted us to join the twenty other states that required *everyone* to use seat restraints. Isaiah and the students made a presentation to the school board that June. They tried to get as many signatures as they could to advocate for safer seatbelt laws in Iowa.

This was just one of the ways Mrs. Whitney brought to life the class Isaiah was taking, and she made it interesting for him. After the school board presentation, they met with a local state senator who was on the transportation committee. Isaiah presented him with one of the research portfolios they had put together. He had practiced his presentation during summer school and had placed small icon cues throughout the portfolio to keep him organized as he spoke. He seriously explained the costs involved with people who sustain brain injuries and the number of brain injuries and deaths that result from people being unrestrained backseat passengers.

The senator was impressed. His committee had been introducing backseat seatbelt legislation for a number of years but with no success. He thought that maybe Isaiah's advocacy would be the extra catalyst this piece of legislation needed to pass. He told him to keep speaking to others about this important issue, and he would contact him when the legislature convened that winter.

Isaiah continued to study with Mrs. Whitney during the summer, working on strategies that would improve his memory skills and reading skills. They celebrated his one-year anniversary from the accident with a cake. Mrs. Whitney had him finish decorating it with his right hand by putting a date on the top of the cake. Inscribed on the rest of it was a line from a Brandon Heath song: "He's not finished with me yet!" How appropriate. God was not finished, and we continued to see progress.

Chapter Nine
Waiting on the Lord

"*I* now pronounce you man and wife."

These were the words we celebrated to as we witnessed the marriage of our son Tony and his new wife Bailey during that same summer of 2009. Bailey, the PICU nurse, who had provided "drugs" to Randy and I that first night in Iowa City was now our daughter-in-law. It was one of the exciting moments in a family's life when we celebrate bringing in a new family member, and perhaps it was made even more meaningful because of all that had happened the past year.

Isaiah was privileged to be the best man, and he did an awesome job on his best man speech, even hand-cuffing the bride and groom together! Of course, it made sense because his brother is a police officer. But he pointed out it was also a visual symbol for them to remember that marriage is forever. Many of the doctors and nurses who had taken care of him were there in attendance, and once he finished his speech, he received a standing ovation.

It was such an exciting time for our family and even more special since Tony and Bailey would be living within four miles of our place so we would get to see them quite often!

Shortly after the wedding, school started and this year that meant a full day of classes for Isaiah. His stamina had improved, but I was still concerned about his ability to remember all his assignments and new concepts being taught in the classroom, especially since he was signed up mostly for regular education classes. I was grateful Mrs. Whitney would continue working with him one on one to help him with his studies. He also had paraprofessionals with him in most classes to assist with notes and assignments.

Isaiah had been elected Vice President of his class and also Vice President of the Student Senate. These were goals of his because he wanted to be able to lead the entire assembly in the Pledge of Allegiance the first day of school and be able to speak on graduation day. I would have liked to have been there to watch him lead the pledge, but he and Stacey said that parents didn't come to that.

The first week of school was probably the toughest for Isaiah. He came home one night, and I can remember the look on his face. He sullenly stood there with a downcast face and in a frustrated voice asked, "Why didn't I put my seatbelt on that day?"

This was the first time I witnessed him being down. It was only for a brief moment, and all I could do was reply that I didn't know the answer but that God wasn't finished with him yet. God would continue to heal him and undoubtedly had a plan to use him. We hugged, and as quickly as his frustration had come, it left.

God in all His mercy was about to lighten Isaiah's mood. Within a week, he was voted by his classmates to be on the Homecoming Court.

Posted September, 2009 by Ranae

You may notice there are some new pictures on here because Isaiah has had quite an eventful week. It is Homecoming at W-SR, and this Monday night was coronation. Isaiah was privileged to be voted onto the Homecoming Court. And Monday night as they announced 2nd runner up and then 1st runner up, Isaiah said he was looking at all the other guys from his class and thinking 'Okay, it could be him or him.' Then he heard the announcer call his name. The high school students had voted him to be their king! What a blessing!

I remembered that one year ago on the 19th, he had said his first words in two months and was missing out on his junior year. Now, one year later, the students have honored him by selecting him as their Homecoming King. I shake my head and can't help but ask, "What else, God? What else do You have in store for this young man?"

The whole week was filled with activities, and each day had a different dress-up day theme. Isaiah and Stacey made the most of each day. On Friday afternoon there was an all-school pep assembly to recognize students in fall sports and activities and to cheer on the football team before the big game that night. It is traditional for the Homecoming Queen and King to give speeches, and Isaiah was expected to speak in front of more than 700 people. Oh, did he practice! It wasn't the longest speech he would ever give, and he was a little nervous, but once again, he received a standing ovation.

School Tube Video of Isaiah's speech
http://www.schooltube.com/video/46643/IsaiahKrull.speech

When the Friday night football game came along, Stacey displayed her school spirit by dressing up in the school's mascot outfit. She did cheers with the cheerleaders and ran along the stands to give high fives to all the young kids sitting along the front row.

Isaiah and Cody helped out the team by encouraging their teammates as they came on and off the field. It was a different role than either of them had anticipated for their senior year, but they would not be caught sitting up in the stands. They wanted to be down on the field, hearing the plays called in, and slapping their teammates on the back for jobs well done.

Half time came, and the principal announced the royal court to the fans. Isaiah walked out with the Homecoming Queen on his arm to fans cheering and fellow students yelling. It was a wonderful moment and a wonderful honor, and Isaiah enjoyed every minute of it.

Right before Christmas, our church was doing a series on "waiting." Mary and Joseph had to wait for this little baby God was sending.

Simeon waited for the Lord to show him the Messiah before he died. And the shepherds waited out in the fields. I felt as though this whole series was for me! I was waiting for life to get back to normal, waiting for Isaiah to be completely healed.

Impatience had set in, and I was feeling down. I was worried about how Isaiah would handle college or if he even *could* handle it. I worried about how much time it took me to help Isaiah and how little time I had to give my husband and other three children. I felt like I was failing at everything and focusing on nothing.

God gently reminded me to take each day at a time and not to worry. He was still on the throne. Nothing had changed. And then this song was sung at one of the church services, and it touched my heart in the way I needed.

> Chorus:
> I'm waiting, I'm waiting on you, Lord, and I'm
> Peaceful. Waiting, though it's not easy, but
> Faithfully I will wait!
> I will move ahead bold and confident
> Taking every step of obedience
> I will serve You while I'm waiting
> I will worship while I'm waiting
> I will not fade, I'll be running the race
> Even while I wait…
>
> By John Waller

If we are so busy with problems that are in front of us, and we allow them to become too large, we tend to miss opportunities God has out there, beyond our own troubles, to help and serve others. I have found that when I am busy helping someone else, my own troubles seem less stressful.

There was so much yet for me to learn, and God was teaching me little by little. People would call who had children with brain injuries and ask me questions about how we handled certain aspects of Isaiah's care. Or, someone would stop us and ask how we were able to handle all the changes in our family. I discovered that the more God used me to reach out to those who were hurting and looking for answers to their own dilemmas, the more I sensed my own healing.

No one is immune from heartache or tragedy. There is not a person on the face of the earth who has not been touched by some sort of pain within their family. Our family was no different. It all comes down to who we run to for help and strength when we are pressed on every side. We can turn inward and become lonely, depressed souls; removing ourselves from friends, family, society, and faith. Or, we can run to our Creator and be renewed in our strength and comforted by Him. This is what I felt held me from becoming depressed and overwhelmed when everything in me wanted to scream out and shut down.

I was waiting--waiting on the LORD. He did not disappoint me!

Christmas was upon us, and I absolutely love the whole season! Okay, I at least wait until after Thanksgiving to put up the tree, but the following day, it goes up! And this season was exciting because this was the first year Tony would be bringing his wife!

Between Tony's police schedule and Bailey's nursing schedule, we had to try to find a day when everyone could make it. Kayla and David arrived early in the morning. Isaiah and Stacey were already at home, so we were only waiting for Tony and Bailey to get home.

After they arrived, we ate our usual Christmas meal that included ham, mashed potatoes and gravy, and the last of the corn on the cob. Eating the last of the corn on the cob had become a tradition, and I always froze some ears just for this occasion.

It doesn't matter how old a person is, it's always exciting to open gifts! Randy tries to stall so that the kids get anxious. Oh, the anticipation! It is always a joy to see the looks on their faces when they get something they have really wanted. Kayla and Isaiah both received a GPS. We hoped this would keep them from getting lost!

When we were finished with the gifts, we noticed there was still one gift bag under the tree. It had *Randy and Ranae* on the card. Bailey said we had to open it together. We proceeded to pull out all the tissue paper until I finally located a package of pacifiers. I was stumped. Tony has been known to pull jokes, too, and I thought this was one of those times until I looked up and noticed Bailey had tears in her eyes.

"Do you mean we are going to be grandparents?" I asked.

"Yes!" Bailey exclaimed through the tears.

It took a few second to sink in, but then we jumped up with excitement to think we were going to be Grandpa and Grandma! It had an odd sound, but we felt so blessed to be adding a new life to the family!

It was a wonderful family time together, and it went by too quickly.

Break was over, and classes started back up for the kids. Isaiah now had over 800 signatures advocating for a youth seatbelt bill that was going through the state senate. True to his word, State Senator Bill Heckroth invited us to make a trip to the state capitol in Des Moines.

Isaiah was very passionate about seeing this bill get passed to help protect others from being killed or injured as he had been. He confided in me that when he thought about the accident, it bothered him that he could have killed Cody or Jordan. They'd had their seatbelts on, but his unrestrained body could have flown forward and hit them or killed them. It's something many people don't realize. Just one unbuckled person can fly through the vehicle and kill or hurt others even though they are buckled in.

We arrived in Des Moines in the morning and planned on meeting up with the senator. I took a quick picture of Isaiah as he walked toward the capitol. He looked so official carrying his briefcase with his laptop in it. He had a video of an accident he was prepared to show anyone who might need proof of the importance of this bill. I don't believe anyone could have convinced Isaiah that this was not an important, life-saving bill.

Senator Heckroth was on the transportation committee and was in favor of seeing a seatbelt law passed to protect Iowans. The senator introduced us to others on the committee, and we were also able to connect with our local State Representative and speak with him about this bill.

The bill was debated on the senate floor and voted on that day. Isaiah and I sat in the gallery and were introduced to the senators. As we heard the senators testify both for and against the bill, it suddenly hit me how big this was! Here were senators debating a potential law that could save lives from injury or death. The committee chairperson spoke passionately about this bill, referencing Isaiah and his accident as just one example of why it was so necessary. He suggested they call it *Isaiah's Law* in honor of the efforts Isaiah had made to draw attention to this bill and its importance.

After all the debating was done, it came time for the vote. We nervously watched as lights on a board began registering their votes. There would be a few in favor and then a few against as we continued to watch with anticipation. And then came the final total: 39 in favor and 9 against! The bill passed, requiring youth 17 years old and younger to be properly restrained in the back of motor vehicles. But we knew it now had to go to the House of Representatives and be voted on there as well.

After the session ended, there were radio commentators, newspaper staff, and senators wanting to speak with Isaiah and learn more about what had happened to him. They informed him that it doesn't always work quite so quickly to introduce a bill and see it passed. I watched and listened as they asked Isaiah about the accident and his recovery. He handled it all with great ease and seemed to be a natural.

When I asked Isaiah if he was nervous talking to all these different people, his reply was simply, "No, they are people, just like me. I shouldn't be alive today, but God has allowed me to live, and I want as many people to know Him as possible, including these people! This new notoriety eventually opened the door to many other opportunities for him to share his story and his faith.

Although the bill took a very circuitous route towards passage, the day in April finally came when he was invited to Des Moines again, this time to witness the governor signing the bill into law. Once again, he and his story were introduced to the press and the people who attended. He stood behind the table and watched Governor Culver sign the new law and smiled proudly as the governor handed him one of the signing pens.

It was a formal, serious affair, but Isaiah just had to lighten things up with his sense of humor. He told the governor that he had initially worked to advocate for a law that would require all Iowa backseat passengers to buckle up, not just kids, and that he would continue to push for that. Then he smiled and said, "Just like another famous governor has said, 'I'll be back!'" It drew a chuckle from the governor and those around him.

I don't think we realized at the time how many youths this would be affecting. It was a law for the entire state of Iowa, and we will never know how many young lives may be saved from injury or death as a result of this law! But each life spared will have been well worth whatever small effort we may have contributed towards the passing of this law.

It seemed so obvious to me that this was just another part of God's plan.

As Isaiah continued to work on finishing his high school classes, he also worked on getting into a local community college. This meant he would have to take the Compass Test. The college provided him with accommodations while taking the test: he was given extended time and a staff member read the test to him. The Americans with Disabilities Act passed in 1990 includes language requiring schools to provide accommodations to students with disabilities. I didn't know this law existed until we needed to use it! It provides assistance with obtaining a degree to people who wouldn't ordinarily be able to attend college.

While Isaiah was in taking the exam, I decided to do some shopping. I was walking around a department store when my cell phone rang. It was the assistant principal from the high school. He informed me that he had given my number to a reporter and I might be getting a call. I told him that was fine. We had decided to walk through any doors the Lord opened for us to share our faith and Isaiah's story.

It wasn't two minutes later when a gentleman called and identified himself as a reporter from the *USA Today* national newspaper. He had been researching seatbelt laws in different states and had come across Isaiah's story on the internet. He was interested in interviewing Isaiah for an article he was working on about the use of seat belts in the backseat of vehicles. You can imagine how surprised I was!

Of course, Isaiah was as calm as ever as he answered the reporter's questions. He always includes that he is simply alive because of God's hand on him. This time would not be different. His story was printed in the August 18, 2010 issue of *USA Today*, on page three, with a picture of him, and right after the front-page story of the return of Brett Favre!

As May of 2010 approached, so did graduation. We were busy with yard work and all those other projects we had been wanting to accomplish before graduation. In Iowa, families of graduates typically host receptions, and we were having ours at our home. So while we were busy preparing, Isaiah was working on his speech.

He was somewhat nervous because there would be a lot of people in attendance to watch his class of 150 seniors graduate from high school. He didn't want to sound dumb. I told him to try to get it memorized as best he could since he was much more fluent when he spoke if he didn't have to read from any notes.

His speech was probably the shortest of the four given that day, but it was definitely the most heartfelt. To watch him up on stage, a young man whose life had almost ended only a year and a half earlier, made me proud but just a bit emotional! He shared from his heart some of the great memories of high school, and he reminded his classmates of the changes and challenges they would face in their futures. He stood boldly and gave glory to his LORD and Savior, Jesus Christ, for saving him. Immediately, the audience burst into applause and rose to its feet!

Never would I have thought this moment would come in which

my son would be able to stand in front of his peers, his educators, his family, and his friends, and so boldly and without hesitation proclaim Christ as his Savior in such a clear and powerful voice. God had stood with him and brought him through a fiery trial and given him back that voice. Now he was using it to give all the glory to the One to whom it belongs in the first place.

Several awards and recognitions continued that year. Right after graduation, Randy and I, Isaiah, and Mrs. Whitney and her husband were invited to speak at a regional convention of the National Exchange Club where Isaiah was honored as their regional A.C.E. Award winner. He received another award during a ceremony at our local community college that recognized the tenth anniversary of the Americans with Disabilities Act. This led to another local television interview for him.

Later that same summer, Isaiah was given an award for People Who Make a Difference from Blank's Children's Hospital in Des Moines for his efforts in helping to pass the youth seatbelt law. As we were leaving the event, two women approached Randy and Isaiah and me and asked if they could speak with us. They offered Isaiah an opportunity to travel across the state of Iowa to conduct school assemblies in which he would share his own story about his accident, inform students about the new seatbelt law, and help promote safety.

His reply was, "Can I share my faith in Jesus?" They said he could as long as he didn't give any altar calls! He laughed and told them Jesus was part of his story, and he would love to travel and help other kids stay safe. He didn't want anyone else to go through what he went through.

For the rest of the school year he traveled with the ThinkFirst Iowa and I Got Caught team. He put together a power point using the pictures I had taken of him in Iowa City and Chicago and used them to help him share his story. When I think about how I first protested taking those pictures but Randy's insistence on it, I'm so thankful he persuaded me. Now Isaiah is able to use them to reach people by sharing a very important message.

That message continued to be shared the summer of 2011 when he was asked to be a camp counselor and speaker at an area church camp. Only now he was able to speak more freely about God's hand in his life as he showed his power point to each new group of campers. With great passion he would speak to the campers about their own need to know Jesus Christ as their own personal Savior. He would share about how no one is guaranteed tomorrow, not even a 16-year-old young man.

Whenever I have those moments of fear, when anxiety creeps in and tries to bring me down, I am reminded of the many miracles God has done in Isaiah.

~

Our care pages continued until the summer of his graduation. It was coming upon the two-year anniversary of the accident, and we decided it was time to sign off. We felt it only appropriate to have Isaiah do his final blog.

Posted July 26, 2010 by Isaiah Krull

This is Isaiah! Tomorrow will be 2 years since the accident that changed my life. Although there have been some struggles, I only think of them for a second until I think, "I should not even be alive."

The reason I am alive is because of the power of Jesus Christ! My favorite verse from His Word is Romans 10:9–10: "That if you confess with your mouth, 'Jesus is LORD,' and believe in your heart that God raised him from the dead, you will be saved. For it is with your heart you believe and are justified, and it is with your mouth you confess and are saved."

This happens once, when you ask him to forgive all your sins. Once you do, you are covered forever. Knowing this has helped me deal with the struggles I have to face. I know that when I get to heaven, I will not have anything wrong with me...no more blind spots or right-side weakness, and no more brain problems!!! What a day of rejoicing that will be! But until then, I will serve the LORD with all my heart!

I was thrilled to speak at graduation on May 30th and walk with my classmates. I just finished taking a class at Hawkeye Community College this past week, and it seems it went well. I'm waiting for my grade!

This will probably be our last blog, and we just wanted to say how grateful

Ranae D. Krull

we have been for all the support you have given me and the family, everything from prayers to encouragement, money, food, and letters.

God continues to work, and I know He's not finished with me yet!
Thank you,
Isaiah Krull

I turn once again to check on Isaiah and on baby Kinnick, Tony and Bailey's little boy, our grandson, who was born August 30, 2010. They both are fine--yes, both of them.

Just part of our story has been told here because we know that God is not finished yet! Yes, Isaiah still has a gait to his walk and a bit of a hard time recalling certain words. He still has blind spots, and his processing is slow. He attempted some college classes with great difficulty. Classmates would have to take notes for him while he used his flip camera to record what the teacher was saying and also what she had written on the board. He has to listen to the lesson three to four times to remember most of the information. At this time he has decided to put college on hold to pursue what God has put on his heart and that is working at camp.

Although running is a little too difficult, he can seemingly walk for hours. He told his dad he would swim again, he has. And when I think how desperately I prayed for him to find his voice, well, he certainly has! And he is not afraid to use his voice to talk to others about the importance of having a personal relationship with Jesus Christ. God has blessed him with a positive attitude and a zest for life that is contagious, and he has already influenced so many. I have a feeling that will continue for a long, long time.

So you may wonder if I think God has answered my prayers. I can assure you He has and has gone far beyond them in many ways! He doesn't always answer the way we may think He should, but He always answers. And we are all forever changed through Jesus allowing this accident to stretch our family's faith.

I am amazed at God's perfect providence through all our family has endured and survived, and we know we are not alone. Bad things happen, but God takes the bad things and brings new life, teaching us what it really means to trust Him completely and growing us in our faith. We are then able to turn around and comfort others as we have been comforted by Him, our Strong Tower.

Just this past week Isaiah sat down at our kitchen table, a place where many conversations have been spoken, he looked at me with a surreal expression on his face and proceeded to tell me of the thoughts that crossed his mind as he lay in his bed the previous night. He shared, "If God asked me if I could go back to the day of the accident and change it, would I?"

I asked him what his answer would be if he could be able to attend college or become an international airline pilot like he had wanted, would he desire that life back?

His reply, "No! I have been able to share the gospel with so many people since my accident and so many have come to know Christ as their Savior which is for eternity. I would never have had the opportunity to share the gospel with so many people if I was just an airline pilot hauling people around the world."

As a mother there is no greater joy than to hear a young twenty-year-old proclaim such a mature statement of fact. Brain injury and all he gets it! I have to continue to thank Jesus for all the people who diligently prayed Isaiah back to where he is today..

I want to close with the very first verses God gave me in the PICU when we weren't sure if Isaiah would live or not. My prayer is this: that our story will give comfort to families going through hardship, will give hope to those who are down, and will encourage everyone to stand on God's Word and trust in His promises. Yes, life can be hard, but God is FAITHFUL and will uphold us if we allow Him to.

Praise and Glory to Him forever!

Isaiah 40:28-30 (NIV)

Do you not know?
Have you not heard?
The LORD is the everlasting God,
The Creator of the ends of the earth.
He will not grow tired or weary,
And his understanding no one can fathom.
He gives strength to the weary
And increases the power of the weak.
Even youths grow tired and weary,
Young men stumble and fall;
But those who hope in the LORD
Will renew their strength
They will soar on wings like eagles;
They WILL RUN and not grow weary
They WILL WALK and not be faint.

About the Author

Ranae lives in Iowa with her best friend and husband, Randy. They have been married for almost 30 years. They have four beautiful children, two who are married and two at home yet. They have been blessed with two adorable grandchildren and they are a blessing!

Ranae came to accept the work Jesus did for her on the cross at the age of twenty-five. Her life changed and she wanted to serve Him however He wanted. Ranae has been blessed to serve as a small group leader, puppeteer, marriage mentor and lobby host at her church.

Ranae has been blessed to be able to homeschool their four children and operate her own photo studio.

When they were launched into this great trial and did not know what the outcome would look like one thing they did know was that they were not alone. God has shown Himself to be faithful in so many different ways. He has strengthened their faith in taking Him at His Word. No one is immune from struggles in this life but we can take heart by knowing these are only momentary. Her prayer is that this would encourage you as you search the Scriptures to see for yourself that He is more than sufficient in all things.

God bless you and encourage you in your own walk of faith.

Made in the USA
Lexington, KY
06 January 2013